# PRIMER
*for the*
# PSYCHOTHERAPIST

# PRIMER
## *for the*
# PSYCHOTHERAPIST

**Second Edition**

**JOYCE A. BOCKAR, M.D.**

*Department of Psychiatry*
*Norwalk Hospital*
*Stamford, Connecticut*

*formerly*
PRIMER FOR THE NONMEDICAL PSYCHOTHERAPIST

**SP MEDICAL & SCIENTIFIC BOOKS**

New York

SPECTRUM PUBLICATIONS, INC.
175-20 Wexford Terrace
Jamaica, N.Y. 11432

**Library of Congress Cataloging in Publication Data**

Bockar, Joyce A.
Primer for the psychotherapist.

Bibliography: p.
Includes index.
1. Psychotherapy. I. Title. [DNLM: 1. Diagnosis. 2. Mental disorders--Diagnosis. 3. Mental disorders--Drug therapy. 4. Psychopharmacology. 5. Psychotherapy. WM 402 B665p]
RC480.B6 616.89'14 81-5798
ISBN 0-89335-127-X AACR2

# *Preface*

This book is written with the belief that nonmedical psychotherapists will and should be doing the vast majority of psychotherapy in the near future. The need for counseling or psychotherapy is steadily increasing in our fast-changing society. The number of psychiatrists cannot keep pace with this increasing demand for psychological services, to which the increasing number of nonmedical practitioners attests. Additionally, for M.D.s to engage exclusively in psychotherapy seems a phenomenal waste of medical training. On the other hand, it is of the utmost importance that people who think themselves in need of psychotherapy be given a thorough medical screening before embarking on their treatment, to insure that they do not have a medical, surgical or neurological disease in the guise of a psychological difficulty. It is with the knowledge that it is unlikely that the hundreds of patients coming to nonmedical therapists will have received this medical screening that that this book was written. The book is also written in the hope and belief that nonmedical practitioners, given a little of what I call "medical intelligence"—which is in essence a high index of suspicion—will be able to detect signs which indicate the patient should be sent to an M.D. for further investigation.

The difference between a psychiatrist and a nonmedical practitioner of psychotherapy is that the psychiatrist's medical training, both consciously and unconsciously, alerts him to cues that the patient often gives, that some medical disease may be in progress and may be responsible for the psychological complaints. Furthermore, and most important, the psychiatrist knows what questions to ask to eliminate or decrease the suspicion of the medical possibilities which cross his mind. Even so, most of the diseases which could be confused with psychological illness are uncommon, or downright rare. However, it is truly a tragedy when medical disease of this nature is missed and the patient spends a great deal of time, effort and money with no relief of his sympotomatology through psychotherapy.

In the first section of this book, chapters are devoted to describing the most common psychological syndromes seen in the everyday practice of psychotherapy. They are coupled with descriptions of certain medical diseases, most of which, although uncommon, are curable by medical or surgical intervention. The types of questions an M.D. might ask the patient are included with each description so that the nonmedical practitioner can try to eliminate the probability of that specific illness, much the way an M.D. would. Naturally, not all questions which could give medical cues can be included, nor does the first section attempt to make the nonmedical practitioner an M.D. What it does do, I hope, is raise the index of suspicion of the lay professional so that he can "sniff out" possibilities that should alert him to get the patient to an M.D.

The second section of this book aims to give the lay professional specific knowledge of drugs, both prescription and illicit, that are most commonly used by patients with whom he comes in contact. Many of these drugs are prescribed by the referring, consulting or supervising M.D.s with whom most lay professionals are associated. It is written with the realization that often the prescribing M.D. does not see the patient again for a long time. The lay professional is often left, therefore, in a quandary, not knowing if new symptoms are side effects of the prescribed drugs, or how to deal with the very frequent patient complaints about dosage, timing or mixture with other drugs or alcohol.

Certain drugs have proven in study after study that they are more effective than psychotherapy alone (see phenothiazines.) It is the author's opinion that drugs plus psychotherapy are more effective than either alone, and that drugs to relieve anxiety and depression should be used in almost every case where significant syndromes of that nature exist. Familiarizing the nonmedical practitioner with these medications will, it is to be hoped, increase the likelihood that he will see these drugs as an adjunct to his practice. Furthermore, it will give him sufficient knowledge to be able to suggest to his "backup" M.D. which class of drugs he thinks the patient should be prescribed. It should enable him to distinguish certain side effects from psychological symptoms. Most important, it will enable him to know when to send the patient back to the prescribing M.D. for a re-evaluation of the medication or its dosage. Also included in the second section are several of the illicit drugs now in increasingly common usage among younger patients, and several of the abused prescription drugs such as barbiturates and amphetamines whose abuse continues by all age groups. Since no drug is more abused than alcohol, a separate chapter on alcohol and alcoholic syndromes has been included. By including descriptions of effects, addiction syndromes and withdrawal syndromes, the lay professional is in a more knowledgeable position to decide when and if his patient needs hospitalization for these problems.

In summary, this book is dedicated to the patient and to his protection. It is written with the realization that, increasingly in the present and surely in the future, the vast number of patients in need of counseling or psychotherapy will be handled by psychologists, social workers, lay analysts, psychiatric nurses, chaplains, paramedical personnel and indigenous lay workers. This volume is written in the firm belief that the more these lay professionals know about possible medical illness in their patients, and the more they know about prescription and illicit drugs, the more likely it is that the patient will receive the best medical and psychological care.

# Contents

# CHAPTER I

## *Anxiety . . . Or?*

There is a network of nerves in the body called the sympathetic nervous system.* This system is responsible for the physical signs that are associated with acute and sometimes chronic anxiety. The sympathetic nervous system is important in maintaining the integral functioning of the many organ systems in the body. One of the functions of the sympathetic nervous system is preparing the person for "fight or flight." This function is very important because anxiety is the subjective experience that accompanies the body's preparation to run away from danger or stay there and fight it. If the body is going to run or fight, more blood has to go to

*The sympathetic nervous system is really a division of the body's whole nervous system. This division, however, acts often as a whole, and has two common chemicals, one of which mediates the transmission of the final nerve impulse to the receptor nerve cell, and both of which are secreted by the adrenal glands in times of stress. These chemicals are norepinephrine and epinephrine and are discussed in the final chapter.

the muscles, which means that, since there is only a limited supply of blood, it must come from other places. It does. The sympathetic nerves to the intestines cause them to temporarily slow down or stop digestive processes—the familiar "knot" in the stomach. This stopping of the digestive process allows the blood supplying that process to be diverted. Since the body is preparing for possible injury, the blood vessels to the skin constrict, shifting the blood to more vital internal organs and thus insuring that less bleeding will occur from cuts. The released epinephrine from the adrenal glands goes to the lungs and opens up the bronchi (breathing tubes) to allow in more oxygen-containing air at a faster rate. The sympathetic nerves to the heart increase its rate, so the increased oxygen will be pumped to the muscles faster. The pupils dilate, teleologically presumably to be better able to see the danger. Putting all this together, we now have a picture of the patient experiencing or complaining about anxiety attacks.

The patient will state that he gets cold (blood vessels to skin shut down), he begins to sweat, he feels his heart beating more rapidly, he feels shaky and tremulous and his stomach may feel cramped. He may feel nauseous and he may feel the urge to vomit, urinate or defecate. (The expression for anxiety, "I could have shit in my pants," probably comes from this.) The patient may also complain of light-headedness or dizziness, which may be derived from excessive breathing, i.e., hyperventilation, which we will take up shortly. This describes an anxiety "attack," but many people have chronic anxiety and exhibit one or more of the components of the attack almost constantly. They may complain that their hands and feet are always cold, that they have to urinate very frequently, that their stomachs are constantly upset or "in a knot" or that they are frequently dizzy and confused.

Subjective anxiety entails the following conditions: skin cold, sweaty, pupils dilated, hands have a fine, fast tremor (shaking), heart beat is rapid, breathing rapid, digestion slowed, tendency to nausea or vomiting, to defecation or to diarrhea. Remember these signs, since in certain instances if *one* is changed, it may mean medical illness. Furthermore, these signs will serve as a reference for many drug effects, and some withdrawal syndromes, as well as some medical illnesses.

Below is an example of a medical illness, hyperthyroidism, which, from the patients verbal report, mimics anxiety in almost all the respects mentioned except one.

## HYPERTHYROIDISM

Hyperthyroidism is not an uncommon disease. It is caused by overactivity of the thyroid gland, which is located at the base of the neck in front of the larynx. In this disease the patient may complain of feeling anxious, he will be sweaty, he may have a fine tremor of his hands, his heartbeat and breathing are rapid, he tends to have diarrhea. He has all the symptoms of anxiety already discussed, except one: cold. Hyperthyroid patients are *hot.* Their skins are warm to the touch and they may in fact have elevated body temperatures. Hyperthyroid patients have additional symptoms which distinguish them from patients with anxiety, if one remembers to ask. They generally have an increased appetite, but even in the face of increased food intake, they generally lose weight. One of the cardinal questions for this disease, as well as a host of other medical and psychological diseases, is "Have you lost or gained weight recently, and if so, how much and in how long a span of time?" Ten pounds per year is a significant loss or gain. The hair texture of hyperthyroid patients often tends to become finer or thinner. A frequent accompaniment of hyperthyroidism is protrusion of the eyeballs, so that the person looks as if his eyes are too far out of their sockets. One must observe carefully, however, for the black people of certain African origins have naturally protruding eyeballs, and this is merely a racial characteristic.

In short, persons with hyperthyroidism strongly resemble those with a sympathetic reaction, except for the following: (1) they are hot-sweaty, not cold-sweaty; (2) they are losing weight or maintaining weight even in the face of increased appetite and increased food intake (no other disease except untreated diabetes, which does not have the associated sympathetic activity, causes weight loss with increased appetite); and (3) they are constantly in the "anxiety attack" state, whereas the anxious patient is usually not.

Ask the person who is complaining of symptoms that sound like a sympathetic reaction whether he is hot or cold when he is sweaty. If he thinks he is hot when this reaction is going on, or even if he says he is cold or doesn't know, ask further about weight loss and appetite, hair thinning, and if he is continuously in this state (with rapid heartbeat, subjective anxiety and, possibly, shaking). Hyperthyroidism is notorious for producing emotional instability, irritability and manic or depressive behavior. If the hyperthyroidism is severe, a toxic psychosis can occur which can be mistaken for a manic psychosis. Obviously anyone with a psychosis should cause immediate referral to an M.D. or hospital. As a rough guide, a weight loss of ten pounds in one month without dieting should cause immediate medical referral. If any of the patient's answers is cause for question you can suggest he have his thyroid checked by an M.D.

Obviously, not everyone who is chronically anxious exhibits necessarily any of the signs of acute anxiety. Someone chronically anxious may or may not have persistently cold feet or a "knot" in his stomach. The point is that very often patients complain of these symptoms and are quite frightened by them in an acute attack—especially those experiencing hyperventilation. It is comforting in these cases, to both the therapist and the patient, to ascertain that these symptoms are most likely due to anxiety. However, if atypical symptoms develop, refer the patient to an M.D.

## HYPERVENTILATION

Along with their anxiety attacks, many patients tend to hyperventilate—that is, breathe too fast and too deeply for too long. This tends to deplete the body of carbon dioxide which is extremely important in maintaining the pH of body fluids and the form that certain dissolved salts take in the blood (pH is a measure of acidity.) Suffice it to say that when someone hyperventilates the balance of calcium salts in the blood is changed. When this balance is changed, numbness and tingling (paresthesia) of the fingertips, hands and feet, and occasionally of parts further up the extremities, may ensue. (Paresthesia also occurs when one's foot "falls asleep," but for an entirely different reason.) The hyperventilation also causes light-headedness, dizziness, and often pains in the chest, peculiarly enough, around the heart. The patient rarely tells you he is overbreathing. Instead, he complains of numbness and tingling of the extremities, chest or heart pain, light-headedness, etc. He may or may not relate these occurrences to subjective anxiety, and it is highly unlikely he would relate them to specific environmental precipitants. All these symptoms, including the chest pain, disappear spontaneously soon after he stops hyperventilating, and calms down, even if he never realized he was either anxious or hyperventilating.

There are several medical diseases which have many symptoms in common with the hyperventilation syndrome. People who have chronic kidney disease are often irritable, depressed, anxious and chronically nauseous, as well as constipated, and may present themselves to the nonmedical practitioner for therapy for depression or generalized increase in anxiety and irritability before seeing an M.D. Interestingly enough, a derangement in their calcium metabolism also induces numbness and tingling of the extremities, but this generally does not subside as easily as when these symptoms are related to hyperventilation. Be highly suspicious and refer immediately to a doctor anyone who complains of constant, or even intermittent, paresthesia of the extremities.

It is really quite interesting that there is a great difference in probable disease entities if the patient complains of numbness and tingling in one hand or one foot alone. In general, the paresthesias from hyperventilation are most often symmetrical. However, paresthesia starting in the left or right armpit or shoulder and radiating down either arm can signify anything from compression of a nerve root in the neck, to temporarily insufficient blood supply to the heart, causing chest pain (angina pectoris), to an actual heart attack, if accompanied by severe pain or crushing sensation in the chest. Here it is necessary to consider the age and sex of the patient, the frequency, duration, and recurrence of attacks, all of which contribute to determining the likelihood of any of the above problems. In general, hyperventilation is thought to occur somewhat more frequently in younger women, but I have seen a case or two in teenage boys. Heart attacks are rather rare in women before menopause. A man of 45 or older, however, with his first attack of anxiety, profuse sweating, chest pain, and paresthesia of the left or right arm should be immediately suspected of having a heart attack in progress, and he should be seen as an emergency in a hospital or doctor's office. Regardless of sex, if the patient is over 50 and has recurrent attacks of anxiety and pain around the heart, with or without paresthesia, he should be seen by a doctor for further evaluation of what may turn out to be angina pectoris. (A note about age here. Men under 45 and women smokers under 45 are getting heart attacks at an increasing rate. It is wise to refer all patients with symptoms of angina pectoris or with first attacks of the type described above to an M.D.)

To review for a moment, then, the typical patient with anxiety attacks accompanied by hyperventilation is likely to be female, between 12 and 40 years of age. Her attacks may be accompanied by chest pain, symmetrical paresthesia, and light-headedness, all of which disappear rapidly when the attack is over. Nerve root compression, angina pectoris, and heart attacks are not pains which readily subside without medical treatment. The paresthesia of these entities are generally not symmetrical, and the chest pain is of much greater intensity. If your patient is less than 45 all three possibilities are less likely. First attacks in either sex over 35 should be suspect, but more so for men. If the symptoms have been occurring for a while before the patient sought therapy, occur variably during the day, are recognized by the patient as having some relationship to subjective anxiety, and most important, disappear spontaneously and rapidly (within 30-60 minutes), then it is most likely that the patient has hyperventilation syndrome. I had a patient like this who was 26, female and swore she was having a heart attack when it occurred. A mild tranquilizer prevented the attacks and aborted them in every instance. This would rarely be true in angina, highly unlikely in nerve root compression, and impossible if a true heart attack were in progress. Although attacks of angina pectoris are accompanied by anxiety and can subside spontaneously, angina pectoris mostly occurs in men over 35 and women usually beyond the menopause.

One further note on this subject. Most patients with hyperventilation syndrome will probably have consulted a doctor about their symptoms. Unfortunately, I have had several patients with this syndrome tell me that the doctor said it was nothing and told them to see a psychiatrist. Patients have a hard time believing that dizziness or light-headedness, chest pain and paresthesia are "nothing," or worse, "psychosomatic." I have found it very helpful to explain to the patient that she is experiencing real symptoms, but that these are due to overbreathing, even if she doesn't realize it. You can tell her that she can prove this to herself by ending the symptoms herself, simply by breathing in and out of a paper bag. That's right. If she holds the bag loosely over her face and breathes into and out of it for a period of time—usually five or ten minutes—she can stop the symptoms. Really the best way to do this is to put the bag over her head and tell her to breathe normally into it. But you need quite a relationship with a patient before you can put a paper bag over her head!

## HYPOGLYCEMIA

There is another syndrome which, although it is quite rare, is indistinguishable from recurrent full-blown anxiety attacks, unless you ask some very specific questions. Even then, only certain blood tests can definitely make the diagnosis. This syndrome is the often discussed and debated hypoglycemia (hypo = low, glycemia = blood sugar). There are two types of hypoglycemia: intermittent and chronic. The chronic form is so rare that it is only mentioned in passing, since people with it have severe medical symptoms which would drive them to see an M.D. immediately, and they would be unlikely to see a nonmedical therapist except in *rare* instances for depresssion. The intermittent form is cause for great controversy. Let me explain a little bit about the regulation of blood sugar. When proteins or carbohydrates are eaten, their breakdown product is ultimately glucose, a particular type of sugar. The glucose stimulates the pancreas to produce and excrete insulin into the blood stream. Insulin helps glucose get into the cells of all the parts of the body, thereby driving glucose out of the bloodstream. Normally there is an exquisite balance between glucose and insulin maintaining the blood sugar at a normal level, but there is a time lag. When food is ingested, the blood sugar goes higher than the fasting level for about one to two hours, then insulin is called forth and the blood sugar may drop a bit below the fasting level and then return to normal. At the point of falling below the fasting level, it is normal post-prandial (after meals) hypoglycemia if the blood sugar does not fall below a certain level—this is hotly debated. Now, if the blood sugar does fall too far, an "anxiety attack" will occur in a variable amount of time—usually two to three hours after a meal. Some true hypoglycemics pour out insulin even faster and may experience an attack one hour after a meal. The "attack" is a classic sympathetic reaction appearing as an anxiety attack. Depression also has been said to be caused by hypoglycemia. That is *exceedingly* rare, although true post-prandial hypoglycemics *may* complain of mood lability becuase they get depressed when their blood sugar falls too low.

There are several well published M.D.s who do not believe that this syndrome is at all rare, and they tend to blame a host of psychological ailments on it. The large weight of medical opinion, however, supports the contention that it is truly rare in its pure form. The reason that the symptoms are indistinguishable from an anxiety attack is that, when blood sugar falls too low, the body responds with a sympathetic reaction.

People who really suffer from this disorder may have attacks of inexplicable anxiety and consult a nonmedical therapist. If you ask them what times of day they have anxiety attacks, they are likely to state that they wake up with them. This is because their blood sugar, like that of everyone else, is lowest in the morning, the time separated by the most hours from a mealtime. A very astute patient may have already learned that as soon as he has his orange juice and sweet roll the symptoms subside. Unfortunately, most patients don't make that connection. If you question closely, you may find that he gets "anxiety" attacks at 11:00 A.M. (before lunch), about two or three hours after lunch, before dinner, and about two or three hours after dinner. Human beings are such that we try to make events that happen seem rational to us. So the patient may have some very plausible reasons for his distress, particularly if he's been in therapy for a while and has become somewhat more psychologically oriented. There is really no sure-fire way to judge, because even if the patient wakes up with his head pounding, cold and sweaty and shaking, he may still have anxiety—either from dreaming or from having to face an anxiety-producing day. If the symptoms occur *every* morning and *every* day two or three hours after meals (despite the fact that you or the patient feel that he is terrified of a man he sees just before his coffee break), then it is worth checking with an M.D. One further way to determine whether the patient is anxious or hypoglycemic is to tell him to eat sugar in some form (e.g., donut or candy bar) when he feels these "anxiety" attacks coming on. If this completely relieves the symptoms within ten minutes to a half hour, he may indeed have hypoglycemia. If, on the other hand, probably due to the mere suggestion of the therapist, he feels either instantaneous relief or relief only after one hour or more, it is very doubtful that he has hypoglycemia. However, it is certainly worth having him take the diagnostic tests if the patient has persistent recurrent anxiety attacks, occurring at a fairly specific time of day—especially in the morning before breakfast—which are unabated by psychotherapy or tranquilizers for a period greater than two months. (A word about relief by tranquilizers. Although it is possible for tranquilizers to temporarily relieve most of the symptoms, in true hypoglycemia complete relief can only be obtained by eating some form of sugar.) Be suspicious, but remember hypoglycemia is rare.

## POSTCONCUSSION SYNDROME

Subjective anxiety, irritability, increased sensitivity to noise, light, heat or other environmental stimuli, fatigability, insomnia, headaches, and difficulty in concentrating can all be due to psychological disturbances. They can also be the results of a head injury, whether mild or severe, with or without unconsciousness accompanying the injury. It is always necessary, therefore, to ask a new patient whether he has had a head injury or whiplash injury within the last year or two, because the most common presenting symptom of this syndrome is *anxiety*.

It is impossible to separate out the psychological reactions to a head injury from those reactions due to injury to the brain itself. Sometimes the accident triggers off a whole neurotic reaction in which many of the above symptoms are present. The longer the time between the accident and the initiation of symptoms the more likely it is that you are dealing with neurotic symptoms and not the direct results of brain injury.

Persistent headaches which are aggravated by changes in posture, such as stooping or bending over, point to changes due to brain injury. Memory loss for incidents one to two hours before the injury is common if consciousness was lost. Amnesia for periods of years prior to the injury is exceedingly rare and should be suspected of being hysterical (not medical).

Frequently the anxiety and other symptoms do not appear for one to two weeks after a minor injury, and the patient may not make the connection between a minor accident and his sudden development of symptoms. It is always wise if a history of head injury or whiplash is obtained to refer the patient to an M.D. before continuing psychotherapy.

Interestingly enough, the treatment for this syndrome is still supportive psychotherapy and mild tranquilizers, even if the symptoms are found to be due to brain injury. The patient with difficulty concentrating and fatigability needs encouragement to engage in his former activities and work, and he needs reassurance that the symptoms will subside in time.

## TUBERCULOSIS

Although the incidence of TB is declining in the United States, it is still prevalent in underprivileged areas and among alcoholics.

When I was working the emergency room in psychiatry one evening, an alcoholic was sent to me, not because he had a problem with his alcoholism, but because he had vague pain in the upper right side of his chest. (Why this should be cause for him to be told to see the psychiatrist remains a mystery.) This patient said he had a pain in the upper right side of his chest which hurt when he breathed in deeply. I asked if he had lost weight recently. Indeed, he had lost 15 pounds in the last two months. I asked if he had night sweats, where he would almost drench the bed, and he replied that he often had to get up during the night to change his pajamas due to their wetness from sweating. He also said he had been more tired lately, and had a cough which he said he always had and which he attributed to excessive smoking. I ordered a chest x-ray. The patient had TB.

The preceding note about TB is included in this chapter on anxiety because of the association of night sweating with both entities. Chronically anxious patients often awake in a cold sweat in the middle of the night. Their anxiety often makes them persistently fatigued during the day. The triad of night sweating, chronic fatigue, and recent weight loss should alert you to send the patient for a check-up before treating him for anxiety.

## PHEOCHROMOCYTOMA

A pheochromocytoma is a type of tumor which elaborates epinephrine and norepinephrine—the chemicals which participate in the making of a sympathetic reaction and an anxiety reaction, discussed earlier in this chapter. It is an *extremely* rare tumor, but symptomatically presents itself as anxiety, excessive sweating, and headaches—a not uncommon psychological triad. Further manifestations are, again, those described for anxiety states: subjective nervousness, tremors, rapid heartbeat, nausea, weakness, and occasional chest or abdominal pain.

In general, someone complaining of persistent headaches along with symptoms of anxiety should be referred to an M.D.

*You can never be 100 percent certain* (always think tumor)! I once had a patient who complained of extremely short bouts of anxiety, occurring almost daily, lasting five minutes or so. She could never pinpint exactly what set these off, but while they lasted she was terribly distressed and somewhat confused. She had been from doctor to doctor for over a year, and every one of them had told her to see a psychiatrist. Finally, she remembered to tell one astute M.D. that she smelled something funny before each attack and that she noticed that the vision in her right eye wasn't as good as it used to be. It turned out she had a brain tumor whose first manifestation was anxiety attacks.

There are many other medical and/or neurological diseases which have anxiety symptoms included in the picture. Generally speaking, therefore, it is a good idea for all patients to have a general medical checkup early in the course of their psychotherapy.

# CHAPTER II

## *Psychophysiologic Disorders*

The term psychosomatic is used commonly, and is thought by the general public to be a disorder that is "all in your head." The term is often used incorrectly to describe almost delusional ideas or bodily complaints for which no medical basis can be found. The term psychophysiological better describes the complex interaction of psychological and physiological factors which make up these disorders. Psychophysiologic disorders are defined in the *Diagnostic and Statistical Manual of the American Psychiatric Association* as *physical* disorders which have psychological contributors. We have already come across a disorder which is considered to be psychophysiological, namely, the hyperventilation syndrome. There, as in the case of the disorders discussed in this chapter, psychological factors play a role in producing a state of altered physiology in the body. In other words, psychophysiological disorders are "real" in the sense that they have actual physical SIGNS of disease (such as the real ulcer hole in the stomach lining) and actual physical SYMPTOMS (such as tension headache or extreme difficulty in breathing, as in asthma) which are produced by altered physiology in the body. These disorders are recognized as having heavy psychological components, but it has NEVER been demonstrated that psychological factors ALONE can cause any of them.

Psychological stress is known to be able to set off (as in asthma) or considerably aggravate the underlying physical or physiological condition which predisposes the individual to the disorder in question. Let me repeat, however, that psychological factors *alone* are not solely responsible for psychophysiological diseases, nor can these conditions be treated by psychological means alone. Psychotherapy can help reduce the frequency of asthmatic attacks or attacks of ulcerative colitis, but the therapist, and indeed the patient, should always remain in communication with the patient's medical doctor. In order to better understand psychophysiologic diseases, it is helpful to know that there is another network of nerves in the body known as the parasympathetic nervous system.* The neurotransmitter for this whole system is acetylcholine, hence the term cholinergic system (choline = abbreviation for acetylcholine; ergic = moved by). The functions of the cholinergic system involve: slowing the heart rate; decreasing the diameter of the bronchi (breathing tubes); regulating the amount of stomach acid; keeping the food moving through the intestines (by consecutively constricting and relaxing section after section of the intestines (peristalsis); maintaining an erection; and opening urinary and anal sphincters to allow urination and defecation. There are many other functions but they do not concern us here.

It is interesting that one very large and long nerve which originates in the brain controls many of the functions we have just mentioned. This is the vagus nerve and its branches which supply the heart, stomach, and all of the intestines up until the last half of the "large intestine" (colon). Other

*The parasympathetic nervous system, like the sympathetic system, is really a part of the body's whole nervous system, but it too can be affected as a whole (by various drugs or psychological reactions).

parasympathetic nerves which originate in the spinal cord control erection (to a certain extent) and bladder and bowel elimination. This is valuable knowledge since many drugs, especially major tranquilizers (see Chapter 9) and certain antidepressants of the tricyclic type (see Chapter 10) are *anti*cholinergic. That is, they interfere with the functioning of the cholinergic system and cause such things as rapid heart rate, constipation, inability to get an erection, and difficulty in starting urination, to name a few. These anticholinergic side effects of the tranquilizers and antidepressants will be taken up again with their respective drugs. However, it is also important for you to know about the parasympathetic (cholinergic) system for another reason, and that is that *emotions* and thoughts can affect the system, particularly the vagus nerve, and can contribute to the development of ulcers and ulcerative colitis, "irritable colon" syndrome, and asthma, which are generally considered the major psychophysiologic disorders.

Other physical diseases which the *"Diagnostic and Statistical Manual"* (DSM III) of the American Psychiatric Association notes have psychological contributors are: obesity, migraine, headache, painful menstruation (the DSM III was written by men), rheumatoid arthritis, hyperthyroidism (!), regional enteritis and more.

In general, the parasympathetic and sympathetic nervous systems are antagonistic in the actions they produce. Whereas pulses along the parasympathetic fibers to the heart, for example, can cause it to slow down, a sympathetic pulsing can cause increased heart rate. This principle can be used pharmacologically in very elegant ways to control some of the symptoms of the diseases which are about to be discussed.

## ASTHMA

Asthma is a very complex psychophysiologic disorder. It is generally agreed that psychological stress can trigger off an asthmatic attack, but the patient has many physiological predispositions which are highly contributory. Often the asthmatic patient is predisposed to allergies of many kinds, and contact with any substance to which he is allergic can also trigger an attack in the absence of psychological stress. An asthmatic attack is an extremely anxiety-producing experience in and of itself because the patient feels that he cannot breathe, that he is suffocating and is going to die. What actually happens is that there is severe constriction of the bronchi. The drug used to treat an acute attack is a *sympathetic* nervous system stimulant, epinephrine—which, you may remember, is secreted by the adrenal glands in times of stress and causes a sympathetic reaction one component of which is opening of the bronchi. For the same reason, drugs used to prevent asthmatic attacks often contain sympathetic stimulants; these can make an asthmatic patient chronically irritable, nervous, anxious, and insomniac. It is therefore terribly important that the asthmatic patient be asked what, if any, medications he is taking for asthma before assuming he has excessive anxiety. Unfortunately, many asthmatic patients are quite chronically anxious anyway. It is best that the asthmatic's doctor prescribe minor tranquilizers like chlordiazepoxide (Librium) or diazepam (Valium) because major ones (phenothiazines, see Chapter 9) tend to cause constriction of the bronchi and predispose the taker to more asthmatic attacks.

As you can see, treating asthmatics is very tricky and should really be jointly handled by a psychiatrist and an internist. However, when working with an asthmatic patient you should be alert to the anxiety-causing properties of antiasthmatic medicines and the asthma-attack predisposing potential of major tranquilizers and antidepressants. It is also necessary to realize and also inform the patient that psychotherapy itself can temporarily cause stress which may further aggravate asthmatic attacks.

## ULCERS

An ulcer is an erosion of part of the lining of the stomach or the duodenum (part of the intestine just after the stomach). An ulcer is really quite small, often less than one-half inch in diameter. One of its characteristic symptoms is that eating most foods (except spices and onions, etc.), especially milk-derived foods, relieves the chronic pain which is usually located on the right side or midline, just below the rib cage. Ulcers are also a very complex psychophysiologic disorder. It is known that ulcer patients have a higher amount of acid in their stomachs than the rest of the population. All the mechanisms which come together to cause an ulcer are not yet fully understood, but one highly contributory factor apears to be overactivity of the vagus nerve's branches to the stomach. (If you remember, the vagus nerve originates in the brain and by extremely complex mechanisms is influenced by thought and emotion.) The surgeon often cuts the vagus nerve's branches to the stomach if an operation is necessary for an ulcer. In this case the anticholinergic properties of major tranquilizers and antidepressants are in the patient's favor, but the gastric (stomach) irritation produced by those drugs themselves are not. Again patients with ulcers are probably better off with minor tranquilizers, if tranquilizers are necessary.

Ulcers can bleed if the erosion hits a blood vessel. If the bleeding is slow but significant *over time* the patient may begin to complain of weakness, fatigue, depression or anxiety *which are also signs of anemia.* Be alert to this if your patient *has* an ulcer or has *ever* had one, since ulcers are prone to recurrence even though they heal. A patient with a history of an ulcer who keeps his appointment with you having awakened with severe anxiety, rapid heart rate, cold sweating, weakness and/or nausea, and who, *if you remember to ask,* admits to having had a black, tarry, diarrhea-like stool that morning should be taken to a hospital, since he is showing signs of acute blood loss. (In this case the sympathetic reaction was set off by severe blood loss.) Many neurotic ulcer patients get into psychological panics and severe anxiety reactions which have the same symptoms as just described for acute blood loss. In this situation check with the patient about having a black, unformed bowel movement or vomiting blood. If neither has occurred it is unlikely that the patient is suffering severe blood loss. The slow blood loss causing anemia is a little trickier, since it might not be noticed in the stool, and all that remains is fatigue, depression, and other "psychological" symptoms. It is always wise to have the patient with an ulcer history, who complains of fatigue and depression, check with his internist before continuing or initiating either psychotherapy or antidepressants.

## ULCERATIVE COLITIS

Ulcerative colitis is a condition of small ulcerations and severe inflammation of the colon (large intestine). It is characterized by intermittent bouts, lasting days to months, of constant diarrhea which is often bloody. Psychological and physiological components both play major roles in this disorder. It can be debilitating and can lead to death by several mechanisms. The patient currently with this disease, or even with a history of it, who wants psychotherapy *must* be treated by a psychiatrist and an internist simultaneously, and no non-medical psychotherapist should undertake treatment of such a patient.* Psychotherapy is, of necessity, often very stressful to the patient. This could set off a fulminating attack of quiescent ulcerative colitis which could end in severe physical debilitation of the patient, if not bring him close to death.

## IMPOTENCE

Never assume that impotence is psychologically caused until the man has been checked out thoroughly by a doctor. There are some screening medical questions you can ask which may save a lot of time. Of course, a good psychosexual history is in order.

*This really has to do with the sociology of medicine in the sense that it is usually easier for an M.D. to keep in constant communication with another M.D. than it is for a lay therapist to do so. If, however, there is very good continuous communication between you and the patient's internist, it is certainly acceptable to initiate psychotherapy.

The maintenance of an erection is a psychophysiologic function involving the parasympathetic (cholinergic) nervous system. The ability to ejaculate is a psychophysiologic function involving the sympathetic nervous system. In the strict sense of the terms, the inability to achieve or maintain an erection is known as impotence, and the inability to ejaculate is known as ejaculatory incompetence. If a patient is complaining of either of these problems, the *first thing* to ask him is about his *intake* of *alcohol* and/or drugs or medicines. The most common cause of sudden impotence in a previously potent man is over-indulgence in alcohol. Alcohol, by many mechanisms, can prevent erection, and a cycle of impotence is begun in the following way. The man has too much to drink one night, wants to have intercourse and finds that he can't get an erection. This is extremely upsetting to him, especially if it is the first time it has ever happened. He vows to try to have intercourse the next night, so beforehand, to calm himself he has a few shots, maybe a few too many, and lo and behold, "it won't work" again. After that, he is so worried that "it" won't "work," he can't (sometimes) get an erection, even without the alcohol, and comes to a therapist in a panic. Thus, it is always advisable to ask such a patient how much liquor he usually drinks before attempting intercourse, and especially how much he drank the night that his erective competence first failed. Theoretically, many drugs can cause impotence if they have anticholinergic properties. Since phenothiazines are both anticholinergic and antisympathetic they could cause both impotence and ejaculatory incompetence. I have, however, more often heard of difficulty in ejaculation than difficulty with erection. The anticholinergic properties seem to be taken out on the urinary sphincter, since difficulty in starting urination is another common complaint with phenothiazines and tricyclic anti-depressants.

Impotence can also result from a host of medical and neurological diseases such as diabetes, alcoholic neuropathy, advanced syphilis, multiple sclerosis, and many others. Therefore, it is a good idea to have the patient checked out medically before proceeding with psychotherapy.

Heroin is a notorious cause for impotence or delayed or completely inhibited ejaculation. Another occurrence reported with certain phenothiazines is that a man has an orgasm but no semen is emitted—this can really be cause for panic in a person already in need of major tranquilizers. What may happen is that occasionally there may occur a retrograde ejaculation back into the man's bladder rather than out through his penis. That is, for as yet unexplained reasons, the usual direction of the seminal emission is reversed, and the semen is propelled into the bladder rather than out. The gratification of orgasm remains, however, with the exception of the enjoyment derived from the actual sensation of the semen leaving the penis. It so happens that this phenomenon has been more often reported with thioridazine and mesoridazine although it is known to occur with all phenothiazines. Very often there are compelling reasons, however, to use these particular phenothiazines. If this happens to one of your patients, and you can explain that it is a side effect of the drug, and, moreover, remind him that he is still having an orgasm, he may well be willing to live with it. It is also of great importance to reassure him that there is nothing wrong with *him*.

There are as many psychological causes for impotence as there are men who have the difficulty. It is only necessary to realize that there may be drug or alcohol-related causes or medical diseases which need to be ruled out before the sometimes difficult psychotherapeutic job of relieving the impotence is undertaken.

## PREMENSTRUAL TENSION SYNDROME

Mild depression, irritability, headache, fluid retention (water bloating), breast and/or abdominal tenderness a few days to a week before menstruation have a normal physiologic basis. Menstrual cramps not severe enough to require narcotics also have a physiologic basis. The mild depression and cramps, etc. have for too long been considered as neurotic symptoms having as their "unconscious roots" the rejection of feminity by the woman who experiences them. This is nonsense. It is medically and psychologically wrong to consider these symptoms as neurotic—*within reasonable limits.* There are, however, women who, for a variety of either *medical* or *unconscious* reasons, experience unusually severe menstrual cramps and premenstrual symptoms. It is wise to have the woman check with her gynecologist, especially if menstrual cramping is severe enough to incapacitate her from work, etc. Women in our society have been allowed to use this as an excuse for time off, even though it is not necessary. What is meant here is *incapacitating* cramps which prevent the woman from doing whatever she *wants* to do. Women in our society are also allowed to react, or overreact, to pain, so it is difficult to get a good idea how much of a psychological component there is to the pre-menstrual tension syndrome or menstrual cramps, versus how much the symptoms are of true gynecologic origin. If premenstrual "tension" or other symptoms appear to be playing a disproportionate part in the woman's socio-sexual relations, a gynecological examination is definitely in order.

## FRIGIDITY

The "Diagnostic and Statistical Manual" (DSM III) of the American Psychiatric Association labels this as psychosexual dysfunction, which is far better than subsuming it under psychophysiologic disorders. Frigidity is a very complex psychosexual disorder. There can be failure of any arousal at all, which would manifest itself physically as lack of engorgement of the labia and lack of lubrication of the vagina. There can also be arousal with failure to have orgasm, which by itself is a complex psychophysiologic function. If I may interpret some of the deluge of literature on this subject, it seems that the most common cause for either failure of arousal or failure of orgasm is inadequate or improper stimulation. That is, the partners of so-called frigid women may not know how or where or when to sexually stimulate these women. Therefore, in dealing with a so-called frigid woman, a particularly detailed psychosexual history is in order.

It is known that some of the physiologic functions involved in arousal and orgasm are under the control of the sympathetic and parasympathetic nerves of the lower spinal cord, so that any diseases previously listed for men, which affect the lower spinal cord, could affect orgastic capacity in women. These nerves also have endings which supply the uterus. *Small* uterine contractions are therefore a natural part of orgasm. *They in no way endanger a normal pregnancy at any stage.*

Although there are no definitive studies showing the labial and vaginal responses to drugs, I have heard of both major tranquilizers and antidepressants causing a decrease in vaginal lubrication during sexual stimulation. certainly CNS depressants could depress libido and cause frigidity on that psychophysiologic basis. In general, the same warning is given here as was given for men. Never assume a woman is frigid on psychological grounds until she has been checked by her gynecologist and probably *also* her internist. One further note: Never assume a woman is frigid until the pattern of stimulation by her partner is thoroughly detailed.

Certain traits of personality have been linked to inhibited sexual excitement and inhibited orgasm. Histrionic traits in women are associated with the above. There is a slight positive correlation between psychopathology in general and sexual dysfunction. However, many patients have no other manifest psychiatric disorder other than psychosexual dysfunction. Some patients will exhibit anxiety, guilt, frustration and somatic symptoms as a result of their psychosexual dysfunction even though they do not usually link their sexual problems with their anxiety and guilt. It is up to the clinician to sort out anxiety *as a result* of sexual frustration and anxiety *as the cause* of it.

## HEADACHES

There are several types of headache, but here we are concerned with scalp muscle and neck muscle tension headaches. These may persist for days or even weeks or come every day at a particular time. Everyone who complains of headache should be sent to an M.D.

# CHAPTER III

# *Depression*

Feelings of depression are the most commonly encountered complaints in the practice of psychiatry and psychotherapy. There are basically two types of depression, neurotic depressions and drug-treatable depressions, with many subtypes. The two major types are labeled by the American Psychiatric Association as 1) chronic depressive disorder (neurotic depression—my term, depressive personality—their term) or adjustment disorder (reactive depression to some life stressor), and 2) major depressive disorder, either associated or not with manic episodes. I call major depressive disorder and bipolar disorder drug-treatable or biological depressions because drugs have been found to ameliorate the conditions about 70 to 80 percent of the time, a percentage which no self-critical psychotherapist could claim when dealing with these types of depressions. My designation as "biological" depression does not mean that there were no precipitative factors to the depression, as did the term "endogenous," formerly used to designate this type of depression. It merely refers to characteristic disturbances in biological functions such as sleep, appetite and psychomotor activity.

Let us, then, describe a depression. Some of the psychological symptoms are the same for neurotic depression as for major depression. The psychological symptoms of depression are known to all of us from personal experience. They are: loss of interests, loss of the ability to experience pleasure, not caring, withdrawal from previously cathected objects like family or avocation, inability to concentrate, indecisiveness, slow thinking, decrease in energy, fatigue, decreased self-esteem, guilt and suicidal ideations. When these symptoms are alone, without biological signs, and they have persisted for two years, it is given the designation chronic depressive disorder, or if in reaction to some stress, adjustment disorder with depressed mood. The biological signs are: sleep disturbance, usually early morning awakening or intermittent awakening, appetite disturbance and a significant change in weight (one lb. per week or 10 lbs. per year, not dieting), depression worse in the morning, irritability, psychomotor agitation or retardation, and delusions.

A manic episode is characterized by the following symptoms: The person is more active socially, or more talkative, works more or is physically restless, has inflated self-esteem, decreased need for sleep, distractability, irritability, and either flight of ideas or the subjective feeling that thoughts are racing. Usually there is decreased appetite and significant weight loss, although usually-fat people may have increased appetite and weight gain. If this type of episode lasts for a few days or longer, it is considered a manic episode. Manic episodes without a history of depressive episodes are extremely rare. When combined with depressive episodes it is called bipolar affective disorder—better known as manic depressive illness.

Some interesting statistics are: European and American studies indicate that 18–23% of females and 8–11% of males in the United States have had a depressive episode (major depressive disorder) and that 6% of the females and 3% of the males have had a depressive episode requiring hospitalization. It is estimated that from .4–1.2% of the adult population has bipolar affective disorder. Also interesting is that, unlike what was formerly unipolar illness (major depressive disorder), where women predominate, bipolar illness is equally common in males and females. Further, persons with biological signs of either depression or mania have a 20 times greater suicide rate than those without biological signs.

The psychotherapist will want to know what to look for; thus, I will describe some of the more common biologic signs. What are biological signs?: sleep disorders, appetite disorders, and psychomotor symptoms. Each of these will be described below. The important thing to realize is that *depressions with biological signs are quite serious,* and patients with these signs are more likely to respond to drug therapy, which makes it doubly imperative that these patients be referred to a psychiatrist (in preference to general practitioner) for appropriate medication.

## DISORDERS OF SLEEP

### Early morning awakening

The patient, although going to bed at his usual time, wakes up consistently much earlier (two to four hours earlier) than his usual awakening time and *cannot* get back to sleep. This problem alone when in the presence of psychological depression is sufficient to diagnose a drug-treatable depression!

### Intermittent wakefulness

The patient can't stay asleep long, sleeps a few hours, is awake for an hour or two, falls asleep and wakes again. It is important to realize that the total time spent asleep may not be shortened if the patient spends long enough in bed, but his sleep is disrupted.

### Difficulty falling asleep

This can be a sign of anxiety as well as depression and is usually combined with other sleep disturbance in severe depression. Sometimes, in severe depression, all three difficulties are present and the patient has nearly complete insomnia. This alone in the presence of psychological depression is *not* sufficient for diagnosis of drug-treatable depression.

### Hypersomnia

The patient sleeps excessively (9–12 hours) during the night, and often during the day, claiming this to be his only respite from depressed mood. It is important to realize that this type of sleep disorder, along with other biological, psychological and historical signs, can be a *biological sign of depression and not merely an "escapist mechanism."*

## APPETITE DISORDERS

The most usual case in depression and mania is weight loss. Some patients do have weight gain. Some obese manics, when they get manic, go on a diet. They are probably able to do so because of the usual decrease in appetite associated with mania. So, although the books say that a significant weight loss *without dieting is 10 lbs. in a year, don't be misled into discounting a weight loss in a dieting person who is otherwise probably manic.*

## PSYCHOMOTOR SYMPTOMS

### Psychomotor retardation

The patient will have a monotonous facial expression; he may remain in one position for a prolonged period of time (15 minutes or more); he does not use his hands in talking, and they may remain in his lap or on the arms of the chair; his sentences may be halting, with much time elapsing between them or even between words of a sentence. The clinician gets the impression of a general slowness to the patient's thought processes, speech, and movements.

### Psychomotor agitation

More easily observable than retardation, psychomotor agitation involves inability to sit still, pacing, wringing of hands, frequent changes (or contortions) of facial expressions and body positions, and excessive, rapid talking. The clinician here gets the impression of an extreme restlessness, and hyperactivity of the patient's body movements, thought processes, and speech. This is to be distinguished from manic hyperactivity and pressured speech by the mood of the patient and content of her speech.

### Anergia

This differs somewhat from psychomotor retardation, in that the person shows severe lack of energy. The slightest usual act like brushing hair may be felt to be too much to accomplish for the patient with this symptom. The patient with retardation, however, will brush her hair, but *very* slowly.

## OTHER PSYCHOBIOLOGICAL SIGNS

### Loss of libido

Usually this means loss of sexual interest, but it may be accompanied by impotence or frigidity as well. In a broader sense it refers to loss of interest in most things in the world outside the self, a loss of emotional investment in people, activities, etc.

### Anhedonia

This is a bit different from loss of libido, although it does overlap with it. It is the inability to experience pleasure from any source, as well as the loss of the pleasure-seeking drive. People with this symptom literally can't think of anything that would give them pleasure, nor do they experience pleasure from any person or activity.

**Criteria for depression**

The criteria for severity of a depressive episode are: moderate, the patient must have four (4) of the following symptoms.

1. weight loss or weight gain of 10 lbs. in one year.
2. early morning awakening or intermittent awakening or hypersomnia.
3. loss of energy, fatigue.
4. psychomotor agitation or retardation.
5. loss of interest or pleasure in usual activities.
6. loss of libido.
7. feelings of self-reproach or excessive guilt.
8. complaints of inability to think or concentrate or indecisiveness.
9. recurrent thoughts of death or suicide.
10. reverse diurnal mood cycle

For a markedly severe depressive episode a preoccupation with suicide or three of the first five criteria listed must be present.

Sometimes patients who have suicidal thoughts will hide them. But suicidal thoughts are so common, so prevalent if a person has biological signs of depression (sleep, weight, psychomotor and energy decrease) that, if you come across someone who has biological signs, you must not only remember to ask about suicide, but suspect the person of harboring these thoughts with the intention of acting on them if they are denied.

One further note about biological signs. Sleep disorders can be masked if the patient regularly uses alcohol, sleeping-pills or narcotics. Even the psychological extent of the depression can be masked by the temporary euphoric effect of alcohol or narcotics. The worst thing about alcohol, sleeping-pills, and narcotics in depression is that they increase the depression, although the patient may continue to take them for the *temporary* relief they afford. *Therefore, be especially alert to the patient who has increased his use of these drugs while continuing to complain of psychological symptoms of depression,* even if he has no evident sleep or appetite disorder.

## BRIEF CLASSIFICATION OF DEPRESSIONS

There are five major categories of affective disorder: major depressive disorder, manic disorder, bipolar affective disorder, schizoaffective disorder, and chronic depressive disorder. Major depressive disorder is characterized as above. There is small evidence that hypersomnia and anergia and weight gain may represent a bipolar type of depression, but sleep loss–weight loss depressions are also seen in bipolar illness. Manic disorder alone is rare, but manic depressive illness usually starts with a manic episode. Schizoaffective disorder is the presence of schizophrenic symptoms during an affective episode. These particular schizophrenic symptoms involve delusions of alien control, thought broadcasting, auditory hallucinations, preoccupation with a delusion to the exclusion of other concerns, and delusions of guilt, sin, poverty, nihilism or self-deprecation in the presence of manic or depressive symptoms. (See section on schizophrenia.)

A severe manic may appear schizophrenic, and an excited catatonic patient may appear manic. I have had experience with two depressed patients who fulfilled the criteria for major depressive disorder, showing no schizophrenic features, but who were really schizophrenic, which became overt when they were given antidepressants. (Antidepressants have the capacity to activate an underlying schizophrenia.) It is chronic depressive disorder (depressive personality) (neurotic depression) and adjustment disorder with depressed mood that must be distinguished from major depressive disorder, bipolar disorder and cyclothymic personality.

Now, all of us have periods of depression and all of us have periods of good mood or even high mood. What distinguishes us from persons with affective disorder? First of all, in depressive personality, the symptoms must be pervasive but sometimes intermittent for two years or more. Second, the periods of normal mood should not exceed two months—otherwise you are heading for major depressive disorder—recurrent. During the depressed periods in depressive personality, many of the symptoms (psychological symptoms) of major depressive disorder are present, but the severity of the symptoms and the degree to which social and occupational activities are impaired is less. The "Diagnostic and Statistical Manual" (DSM III) does list some of the "biological" signs of depression as part of the syndrome of depressive personality. They are: insomnia or excessive sleeping and low energy level. Remember that these have to continue, *for the most part,* for two years. The type of insomnia is usually difficulty in falling asleep. The psychological symptoms usually are of greater severity than the biological symptoms. They are: feelings of inadequacy, decreased effectiveness at work or school, concentration problems, loss of libido, pessimism about the future, crying and recurrent thoughts of death or suicide.

It cannot be overemphasized that these symptoms must be present for two years; that the severity of the symptoms does not reach that of major depression disorder; that the severity of impairment is milder than in major depressive disorder; and that the person usually does get to sleep eventually; he does *not* have total insomnia; he does not lose or gain weight (except fat persons); and he does not have psychomotor symptoms. Basically, depressive personality is a concept derived from the old "neurotic depression," and there patients rarely have sustained biological signs. Further, for the most part, you can use the presence of biological signs to distinguish between major depressive disorder and chronic depressive disorder (depressive personality).

So, normal people differ from people with these disorders by the factors of 1) brevity of symptoms, 2) absence of biological signs, 3) brevity of mood swings, and 4) lack of sustained impairment of social, occupational or home activities. But how do normal ups and downs differ from cyclothymic personality? Cyclothymic personality disorder has a greater degree of impairment in social or occupational areas.

There is no clear distinction between cyclothymic personality and mild bipolar illness. The diagnosis is made on the basis of severity of symptoms and degree of impairment in various areas plus chronicity of two years or more. Generally speaking, major depressive disorder and hypomania or mania have relatively sudden onsets and clear endings. The patient with cyclothymic personality does not have clear, abrupt beginnings to his mood changes. Even if the cyclothymic person has a major depressive or manic episode, he will return to his cyclothymic behavior once the episode is over. In his hypomanic periods he may be quite overproductive, whereas in a manic disorder the patient is usually too distracted or irritable to complete projects.

I must give you a clinical example of a patient who was referred to me by a clinical psychologist who suspected manic-depressive illness. Margret (Peggy) is a 45-year-old, white, married woman whose father was a psychiatrist and whose mother was a successful nutritionist who became manic depressive in her later years. Peggy said that she had been depressed for ten years. Before that, she related, every time she went to Europe she would get depressed. (She was a German major in college and had an incomplete masters in German hanging at Yale University for the last 10 years). She said that she had been unable to dust or clean the house in the last two years and that there were piles of clothes, papers, etc. in every room of the house. (Her husband was also depressed and did nothing around the house either.) She described her six-year-old daughter as not doing well either. I asked her if she had had any periods in the last 10 years of normal or increased mood. She denied any high periods but said that she had had one-month periods of normal mood sometime in the past, but not for the last two years. She had been continuously depressed for the past two years. (This is a good place to set up the differential diagnosis. It could be that she has chronic depressive disorder (depressive personality) or major depressive disorder, or even bipolar affective illness.) There is nothing to say how long a major depression lasts, and her home functioning was severely impaired insofar as housework and child rearing were concerned. I asked her about her sleep only to discover that, for two years, she had been going to sleep at 11:30 P.M. and waking at 4 A.M. She had gained 30 lbs. and considered suicide all the time but would not do it because of her daughter. I asked her if she had seen other psychiatrists and if they had given her any medication. She said she had Triavil (antidepressant tranquilizer), but I found out that the dose had been inadequate. Nevertheless, she had had one good high from the Triavil, which unfortunately lasted only 2 days, wherein she returned to being depressed. Given that information, I gave her Elavil (pure antidepressant and one ingredient of Triavil). She responded with a controlled high three weeks later and cleaned up the whole house. This leaves us with two of the original three possibilities. With the presence of clear biological signs—early morning awakening and weight gain—depressive personality is probably excluded. Then we have major depressive disorder or manic depressive disorder, either of which it could be. We also have the possibility of an adjustment disorder with depressed mood if we consider her going-to-Europe-depressions. There is nothing to say that major depressive disorder or bipolar disorder can't be precipitated by life events. An adjustment reaction is too mild for this case, and is too-short lived. I think we have to take into account the family history of manic depressive illness and conclude that Peggy is probably manic-depressive and that this is supported by her high following administration of an antidepressant. (I will take this up under antidepressants.)

Notice that if I did not inquire as to sleep, weight, sex drive, etc. and observe psychomotor behavior I might have come to the conclusion she was a depressive personality. Such is the importance of biological signs. (Incidentally, she also had psychomotor agitation.)

One further note on this subject. Sadness, psychomotor retardation, weight loss, insomnia, mild memory impairment, anergia or chronic fatigue, irritability, and vague or specific somatic complaints can all be signs of an as yet undiscovered physical illness. Medical consultation is imperative in patients with these psychobiological signs and symptoms. The final pages of this chapter present possible alternatives to a diagnosis of depression.

## HYPOTHYROIDISM

Every once in a while I am reminded of the importance of *looking* at a patient. A patient came to me complaining of depression and said she had gained 40 pounds in the last four months. Her sleep pattern was normal and she had no psychomotor symptoms. She was not a binge eater and had never been fat. She was a smoker and had a somewhat deep voice for a woman, which she thought had always been that way. Somewhere out of my previous medical training came the thought of hypothyroidism (probably based on nothing more than the weight gain). Then I took a look at her. She had no hair on the outer third of her eyebrows and no hair on her legs, and she didn't shave or tweeze either. The characteristic changes of hypothyroidism were right there: obesity, loss of leg hair and the peculiarly characteristic loss of eyebrow hair on the outer third of both eyebrows, and a very characteristically deep voice.

Hypothyroidism is *under*activity of the thyroid gland. These patients complain of depression, loss of energy, chronic fatigue or weakness just lilke depressed patients. Also, females may have only a few or no menstrual periods, a symptom consonant with either hypothyroidism or depression. Most people have usually gained a considerable amount of weight, incxplicably, if the disease has been going on for a few months. In additon to the hair losses, deep voice and obesity, they have a tendency to feel cold or be sensitive to cold weather. A good look at your patient and a careful listening to his/her voice in addition to a history of weight gain and depression should alert you to the possibility of hypothyroidism along with the possibility of a clinically significant depression.

## ADDISON'S DISEASE

Addison's Disease is a relatively rare disease of the adrenal glands, and is mentioned very briefly because its onset is characterized by the same psychologocal and biological signs as depression. The one outstanding characteristic to be aware of is a deep tanning of the skin, which occurs with or without exposure to the sun. If you happen to notice a particularly deep tan on a patient who complains of depression, fatigability, anorexia, etc. it wouldn't hurt to check it out with an internist.

## DEPRESSION SECONDARY TO VARIOUS DRUGS

As mentioned, alcohol, sleeping-pills, and narcotics are ultimately depressing drugs even if they produce temporary euphoria. In addition, persons addicted to their use very often have chronic depressions for which they use those drugs. Antidepressants can be used even in the face of alcohol, sleeping-pills or narcotic abuse, but dosage and patient reliability are problems not easily solved.

Not so infrequent causes for depression are drugs used in the treatment of high blood pressure, and this must be kept in mind when a patient complains of depression. The worst offender in this category is Reserpine or drugs derived from Reserpine or containing Reserpine, commonly known as Serpasil, Raudixin, Renese, Regroton, Hydromox, Diupres, etc. These and another antihypertensive, alpha-methyldopa (Aldomet), can cause severe psychological depression in about 15 percent of those persons treated with them, and who may or may not exhibit biological signs. *The importance of asking the patient what drugs or medications he is taking,* before even thinking about psychological causes for his distress, *cannot be overemphasized.* Drugs given as tranquilizers, such as meprobamate (Miltown, Equanil), diazepam (Valium), chlordiazepoxide (Librium), or even phenothiazines (Thorazine, Stelazine, Trilafon, etc.), can cause or worsen depressed mood. Amphetamines (speed), commonly thought to be "ups" or stimulants, are responsible for depression also. It has been shown experimentally that when volunteers were given large doses, they became depressed (before becoming psychotic, I might add). Furthermore, when amphetamine "highs" wear off, the person commonly experiences a "let-down" which can be a severe depression, depending on how high a dose he was taking before he stopped. In street language, the tremendous depression following discontinuance of chronic ingestion of amphetamines is known as "crashing." This type of depression can be quite severe and presents a moderate suicide risk.

In summary, then, depressed mood can occur in a wide variety of psychological and medical situations. Biological signs such as sleep and appetite disorders and psychomotor symptoms occur almost always in clinically significant depressions, and indicate a more serious depression than psychological depression without those signs. The suicide rate among depressives with biological signs is vastly higher than for the general population. Depressions with biological signs require drug therapy even if the signs have only been present for two weeks. (A patient who loses some sleep on one or two nights, however, is not ordinarily an immediate candidate for antidepressants. Nor is the person who has had lifelong feelings of depression without accompanying biological signs.)

Antidepressant drug therapy *works* in the range of 60–70 percent of the time, with some estimates even higher; hence, it is truly tragic to treat a psychobiologically depressed person solely with psychotherapy, when a great deal of his misery could be alleviated in two or three weeks. Such therapy might even prevent a suicide.

# CHAPTER IV

# *Schizophrenia*

Once you have seen a schizophrenic, you know what a schizophrenic is. The "Diagnostic and Statistical Manual" (DSM III) of the American Psychiatric Association recognizes that schizophrenia has certain phases, a prodromal phase, an active phase and a residual phase. It also notes that a return to complete premorbid functioning is rare, but complete recovery does occur. There is one interesting stipulation to the diagnosis of schizophrenia and that is that whatever phases have been passed, the disease must be present for six months. Let us now get to the description of schizophrenia in the acute active phase and in the residual phase.

The DSM III notes 10 symptoms, any *one* of which is sufficient to make the diagnosis of schizophrenia. Obviously, since *one* symptom is sufficient for diagnosis, it is terribly important to establish the presence of that symptom unequivocally. These symptoms are: 1) delusions of being controlled by external forces. The patient may feel that his thoughts, actions, or feelings are being controlled by either the minds of other people, electricity, etc.; 2) thought broadcasting—the subjective feeling that the patient's thoughts are being broadcast from his head to the external world so that other people hear them; 3) thought insertion—the experience of having thoughts which are felt to be inserted in his mind by other powers (other than God); 4) thought withdrawal—the belief that his thoughts have been removed from his head resulting in a diminished number remaining; 5) other bizarre, fantastic delusions of any nature; 6) somatic, grandiose, religious or nihilistic delusions; 7) delusions of *any* type if accompanied by hallucinations of any type; 8) auditory hallucinations in which either a voice keeps up a running commentary to the patient about his behavior or two or more voices converse with each other; 9) auditory hallucinations on several occasions with content having no relationship to depression or elation; 10) either incoherance, loosening of associations, marked illogicity or marked poverty of content of speech—if accompanied by blunted, flat or inappropriate affect or delusions or hallucinations.

The above are symptoms of the active phase. The symptoms of the prodromal phase and the residual phase are the same: 1) social isolation or withdrawal; 2) marked impairment in functioning at work, school or homemaking; 3) markedly eccentric, odd or peculiar behavior like hoarding food, collecting garbage; 4) impairment of personal hygiene and grooming; 5) blunted, flat or inappropriate affect; 6) speech that is tangential, vague, overelaborate or circumstantial; 7) odd or bizarre ideation or magical thinking, superstitiousness, clairvoyance, telepathy, etc.; 8) residual types of nascent delusions or unusual perceptual experiences—nascent hallucinations. The presence of any two of the above symptoms are sufficient to make the diagnosis of schizophrenia in that phase, provided that the total time spent in all phases together is at least six months.

If you have a patient who seems to be in the prodromal phase, with no previous episode like this one, it should raise your index of suspicion for schizophrenia but it should also tell you to think of other diagnoses as well. Organic mental disorders often present features of schizophrenia in the active phase, such as delusions or hallucinations. Particularly drug induced psychoses can be identical with schizophrenia, especially psychoses induced by amphetamines, LSD, and PCP (phencyclidine). I have seen a lot of chronic pot smokers get amotivational syndromes and flattened affect and deterioration of personal hygiene—yet they were not schizophrenic. Always ask about the use of drugs or alcohol in your initial assessment of a patient.

Differentiating a depressed schizophrenic or an excited catatonic from a depressed person or a manic patient is not always easy. In schizoaffective disorder there is the development of a full affective syndrome which precedes or develops concurrently with psychotic symptoms. In schizophrenia by definition, the affective syndrome develops *after* the development of schizophrenic symptoms (the previously common concept of post-psychotic depression).

I must make a distinction here. Psychotic symptoms are *any* hallucinations and *all* delusions. Schizophrenics in the active phase have *characteristic* delusions which are listed with the symptoms for the active phase. Psychotic symptoms—hallucinations and delusions—occur in many other illnesses besides schizophrenia, but those illnesses have characteristic delusions as well if they are psychiatric, and some have characteristic hallucinations if they are toxic or medical.

## TREATMENT

Before the advent of neuroleptic (antipsychotic) drugs, psychotherapy was the only method of treatment available. Therapist Harold Searles spent eight years in the psychotherapy of one schizophrenic. Today, despite the advent of psychotropic drugs, the basic core of most schizophrenics remains unchanged, and it is they who exhibit the residual symptoms despite taking antipsychotic drugs. *But* it is, in my opinion, tantamount to malpractice to treat an acute schizophrenic with psychotherapy alone. Schizophrenics in the active phase MUST be treated with drugs. Not that they are not in need of psychotherapy—they are—but drugs aid in the development of the ability to communicate meaningfully. They decrease the confusion and increase concentration and selective perception (the schizophrenic has trouble with reacting to too many incoming stimuli) and in general make possible a meaningful relationship with the therapist. The drugs used to treat schizophrenia are called phenothiazines or butyrophenones or thioxanthines, and will be taken up in a later chapter.

What are acute episodes of schizophrenia called if they have had no prodromal period that you can discern? They are now called schizophreniform psychoses, and if they last more than six months, the diagnosis is changed to schizophrenia.

## CLASSIFICATION OF SCHIZOPHRENIAS

### Paranoid Schizophrenia

The essential features of this disorder outside of meeting general criteria for schizophrenia are the presence of persecutory delusions or grandiose delusions, or delusions of jealousy and/or hallucinations with a persecutory or grandiose content. It is extremely important to note, these factors and the treatment is influenced by the distinction between grandiose or paranoid manic delusions and paranoid schizophrenic delusions. The two may not be separable in terms of content of delusions, but the affective response to the delusion will probably make the distinction for you. (Frankly, sometimes the distinction can't be made except by the use of drugs.) Phenothiazines will probably help the paranoid schizophrenic feel at least less threatened by his delusions, if not rid him of them for the most part. Manic patients, on the other hand, may be calmed by phenothiazines, but a large amount of "high" affect usually remains. Furthermore, lithium given to a schizophrenic has, as I have seen, made the patient confused and dysphoric. I have not seen lithium do that to normal or other psychiatric patients.

### Hebephrenic or disorganized type of schizophrenia

The essential features of this disorder are marked incoherence and flat, inappropriate or silly affect. Associated features are grimacing, mannerisms and extreme social withdrawal. Generally hebephrenics have a poor premorbid adjustment and therefore a poor prognosis. This is again to be distinguished from manic psychosis with incoherence. This distinction is usually easily made on the basis of premorbid functioning and the therapist's subjective response to the patient besides all the help that your criteria from the DSM III will give you. For example, manics do not have social withdrawal.

### Catatonic subtype of schizophrenia

The DSM III notes that catatonic schizophrenics have a marked disturbance of psychomotor behavior. The symptoms go from excitement to stupor, posturing rigidity or rapid fluctuation between excitement and stupor. The diagnosis is easily made but once again must be distinguished from manic illness if the catatonic is excited. This distinction would be easy because the catatonic fulfills the criteria for schizophrenia—but alas, many manics also have one characteristic which fulfills *one* of the criteria necessary for the diagnosis of schizophrenia. You really don't have to make the definitive diagnosis—send the patient to a psychiatrist immediately since thyrotoxicosis or drug intoxication could be causing what you're seeing. Furthermore, catatonics can die of dehydration, starvation, exhaustion or hyperpyrexia.

### Some Interesting Information

The prevalence of schizophrenia ranges from .2% to 1% of the general population, and schizophrenics are a sizable proportion of all psychotics. Schizophrenia is equally prevalent in males and females. All researchers have found a higher prevalence of schizophrenia among biologically-related family members. This includes studies in which the offspring of schizophrenic parents were raised by normal parents. There is, however, only a small to moderate concordance rate among monozygotic twins which attests to the multiplicity and importance of non-genetic factors in the development of the illness.

For nonmedical therapists and psychiatrists alike, once the medication is started, it is a long, difficult therapeutic job to help the person with residual symptoms. Furthermore, antipsychotic drugs—any and all—flatten affect, worsen depression (except Mellaril) and cause anticholinergic side effects which can be a real basis for delusional thinking. Worse, the drugs sometimes cause sexual dysfunction in males and inability to lubricate in females. No one with a shaky ego needs that. In most of medicine, therapeutic failures usually die of their illness. In psychiatry, many of our patients just continue to suffer, and it is not we who have failed. It is indeed sad that the DSM III feels that few schizophrenic patients fully recover. It is also sad that antipsycotic drugs are really anti-delusions, anti-hallucinations, when the core of schizophrenic thinking, affect, and sometimes behavior, is left untouched. But the drugs do allow speedy recovery from psychosis, whereupon our job begins.

# CHAPTER V

# *Does Your Patient Have "Organic" Brain Disorder?*

The concept of organic brain disorder includes several constellations of symptoms which doctors have come to recognize are associated with *damage to or loss of actual nerve cells* in the brain or disturbance in their transmission of impulses. When the damage, loss or dysfunction is diffuse throughout the brain, certain characteristic symptoms appear which can be recognized as associated with this organic damage. In order to make the diagnosis, however, medical evidence from x-rays, brain scan, CAT scan, EEG, spinal tap, physical examination or knowledge of the history of the etiological agent is necessary. The organic factor may be a primary brain disease or a systemic disease which affects the brain secondarily. It may be a drug or toxic agent currently affecting the brain or having left a residual effect on the brain or the causative factor may be the abrupt withdrawal of a substance upon which the patient was physiologically dependent. (Organic refers to the *organ* involved, specifically, the brain).

These characteristic symptoms occur together often enough to be called a syndrome (constellation of symptoms). They occur together regardless of the cause of the damage to the nerve cells (neurons) if the damage is *diffuse*. If the damage is localized, as in psychomotor seizures, it is given the name of the area involved. (Psychomotor seizures = temporal lobe epilepsy = "uncinate fits." Uncinate refers to the uncus, which is a smaller area within the temporal lobe of the brain.)

Regardless of the cause of known or even unknown damage to the brain, the symptoms are called an organic brain syndrome (OBS for short). *Whenever you find the symptoms of organic brain disease,* it should cause you to *immediately refer the patient to an M.D.,* preferably a *psychiatrist* or *neurologist.*

Diagnosing organic brain disease is easy in some cases but can be confusing in others. For example, acute schizophrenics are often confused, do not know the date, may be disoriented and in general may present many "organic" features. It may not be possible to tell if this is permanent or temporary until the psychotic symptoms are under control. In other cases, where clear metabolic or circulatory disturbances are known to be present or have occurred, or head injury or drug ingestion has clearly preceded the presence of "organic" symptoms, the diagnosis is easier. Especially with regard to organic brain disorders, it is imperative that the patient be questioned about drug and alcohol ingestion.

The cardinal signs of organic brain syndrome involve defects in attention, memory, orientation, judgment, intellect and affect. But deficits in these areas are sometimes not noticed by the patient and sometimes are noticed. Compulsive people, for example, are rather intolerant of any cognitive deficit, and as good compulsives they tend to fear loss of control when they notice these deficits and they get depressed. Or they may try to compensate for their deficit by making extensive lists so as not to forget anything. Paranoid people get more paranoid. In general, the less social, more negative attitudes of people show up when they start becoming "organic."

## IMPAIRMENT OF MEMORY

Memory loss has several components. There is retrograde memory loss which has three components—recent memory, immediate memory and long range memory. And there is anterograde memory loss, which means that the patient cannot form memories in the present, i.e., his memory for most events taking place after the onset of his acute OBS are dim or absent. Part of anterograde memory loss is derived from deficits in attention and concentration which are also part of the organic brain syndrome. Memory loss usually starts with deficits in recent and immediate memory.

The earliest signs of memory impairment may be simply tossed off as absent-mindedness. The person is beginning to forget the most recent events of his life or most recent things he said. Yet, there is often remarkable preservation for past memories in this early phase. The difficulty really seems at first limited to the neurons responsible for learning and retaining the newest information. Later on, difficulty in remembering past events becomes greater, until ultimately little of the past or present is retained.

Depressives of whatever classification, and some neurotics, as well as persons with major psychoses, will complain of difficulty with recent memory. Close questioning, however, will almost always reveal this to be due to difficulties they have been having with concentration— a problem which can also be a sign of organic impairment. Severely depressed persons or others with major psychoses may not even be concentrating enough on the present to be forming their "recent-memory traces" because they are preoccupied with their psychological difficulties. Persons in older age groups may blame their memory difficulties on getting old, when they are really due to depression or other "functional" problems. It is important, therefore, not to assume someone is "organic" based on age alone, and to defer the diagnosis of organicity until the depression or other symptoms have been controlled.

There are several ways of testing these memory functions. Much testing can be accomplished with the taking of the history of the present illness. In other words, as the patient describes his difficulties take note of whether he keeps saying, "I can't remember," with respect to recent events or past events. Hysterics may claim to have forgotten their entire past but be able to perform well on questions designed to test immediate or recent memory. Remember that recent memory loss always precedes long-range memory loss, and total loss of memory for past events occurs almost exclusively in hysteria or in such severe and widespread brain disease that *all* recent or immediate memory is gone. Remember also that deficits in concentration or attention can cause deficits in recent and immediate recall.

## IMPAIRMENT OF ORIENTATION

The earliest signs of orientation impairment are difficulties in remembering time sequences of events, despite the fact that the patient can remember the events themselves. If there is progression of disorientation, the patient will begin to forget the events themselves, or more particularly, where and when the events took place. In general, orientation is divided into three subcategories—time, place, and person. Disorientation to time is an earlier finding, i.e., a more acute finding, than is disorientation to place or person, but more often than not they occur together. Due to perceptual problems during an acute organic brain syndrome (DSM III delerium) the patient may mistake his hospital room for home, and hence is said to be disoriented to place. What is meant by time disorientation is not only the actual time of day, but *what* day, month, season, year it is. Later on, with further impairment, difficulty in knowing where he is or who the examiner is may occur, and ultimately, after almost all functions of memory and orientation have failed, the patient will be unable to tell you who he himself is. There are many degrees of knowing where one is. In general, this question of placement refers to where the patient is at the moment the question is asked. Obviously not just "in a room" or a vague or nonspecific answer, but an answer indicating the title of a place such as a hospital, doctor's office, emergency room, clinic, etc. is desired.

Orientation to person, really means does the patient recognize persons previously known to him by name or correct relationship, and persons unknown to him by title or function. Remember, only after all functions of orientation and memory have failed will a person be unable to tell you who he is. (Hysterics will feign or really be unable to remember who they are, but there will be no consistent pattern of total memory loss and orientation loss to go along with this type of orientation failure.) The cardinal questions to be answered by the patient either directly or in your mind are: Does the patient know what day, month, and year this is, *where* he is, who *you* are—not your name, necessarily, but your functional title (e.g., examiner, nurse, worker, doctor, etc.)—and lastly, who he is. More subtly, does the patient know the sequence of events from yesterday to today which led to his coming to see you (if this is the first interview) or what occurred yesterday. Questions to test orientation are part of the formal mental status as outlined in Chapter 7.

## IMPAIRMENT OF JUDGMENT

Judgment impairment can be subtle or can be the purpose for which the patient has found himself in your office. The problem is difficult to describe since judgment itself is often a value-laden, subjective entity. In general, judgment can be assessed by evaluating whether or not the person violated his own usual code of behavior or values, or whether he did or said something which is not customary for his socioeconomic class. That is pretty broad, and must therefore be tempered by other factors, such as whether the person was deliberately rebelling against these value systems, or whether indeed he was, for example, so euphoric that he bought a $20,000 car when he makes $15,000 per year. Here, however, we are really considering *gross* judgmental impairment, such as not being able to assess that 30 degrees Fahrenheit is sufficiently cold to warrant wearing more than shirt-sleeves. General states of dress or undress are usually functions of judgment. This is often impaired in schizophrenia and therefore by itself should not be considered significant of an OBS. The old, "What would you do if you found a stamped unopened letter in the street?" is really unfair for judgment, but it is a good index of sociopathy. Generally, your assessment of the patient's judgment will have to come from outside sources if his impairment is more subtle than what is described here. It usually involves slow but noticeable inattention to obvious considerations in decision making and may lead to persons beginning to see the patient as unreliable. For example, the patient may have been a cautious businessman who suddenly engages in reckless business adventures.

## IMPAIRMENT OF INTELLECT

Intellect impairment is easily directly testable by proverbs, numbers, similarities, etc. There is difficulty remembering recent events so that names, phone numbers, what the person was doing may be forgotten, leading to cigarettes left burning in ashtrays, water being left running, etc. Essentially, however, a person's vocabulary and interests may decline. He may not be able to intellectually deal with more than one idea simultaneously, which is a cardinal sign of higher intellect regardless of his level of intelligence, as long as it is at least average.

The signs of intellectual impairment may be reported by outside sources, or become subtly evident during discussion with the patient. Impairment of intellect also depends to a great extent upon the environmental demands placed upon the patient. I heard of a case of a scientist who could no longer do higher-order calculus. This was his chief complaint. Obviously, it would be difficult to test this problem if it were the only problem; however, it turned out that ultimately it was not his only sign of impending OBS. With more severe degrees of intellectual impairment, a general impoverishment of speech and *slowing of intellectual functions* become apparent.

For example, a person may correctly be able to subtract 7 from 100 serially, but do it with extreme slowness which can indicate difficulty in holding the question number and the answer number in his head simultaneously. This can also be a problem in memory, i.e., finding it difficult to remember the numbers to be subtracted. Intellectual impairment is sometimes difficult to separate from memory impairment, and sometimes formal testing is required to establish its presence. It is very important to realize that intellectual impairment constitutes a loss of previously acquired intellectual skills, sufficient to interfere with social or occupational pursuits.

## LABILITY OF AFFECT

The first noticeable signs of lability of affect, which is *very* characteristic of organic brain syndromes, is inability to prevent exaggerated emotional responses. For example, the patient or his relatives may complain that he becomes overinvolved with television programs and laughs too hard or cries at the "drop of a hat" at any program. He may become outraged at small annoyances, an uncharacteristic action, and just as suddenly, forgive the annoyance and burst into tears of love for the persons receiving the forgiveness. Later he will show general impoverishment of emotional response, in that things which previously caused a response in him no longer do so, unless it is an exaggerated one in which he cannot control the emotional tone. Whatever personality characteristics a patient had beforehand now also take on an exaggerated quality. He may become paranoid, more obsessive, or more negativistic. In general, the less likeable qualities of our personalities come to the fore when we begin to get "organic."

## DELIRIUM AND DEMENTIA

What has just been described as the organic brain syndrome, namely, deficits in memory, orientation, intellect, judgment and affect, occurs in two forms—one, acute delirium which has other hallmarks such as hallucinations and occasionally delusions, and the other, chronic or progressive dementia in which the prognosis is usually much less favorable and which is considered permanent. Dementia may also be associated with hallucinations or delusions but is not of the same quality as delirium, as will be described.

Delirious patients manifest all the early signs noted for organic brain syndrome. They are disoriented usually only to time, and perhaps place, although very occasionally, to person. Recent memory is impaired far worse than remote memory. Frequently they hallucinate, primarily visually (visual hallucinations are more often associated with organic impairment than are auditory hallucinations), but if illicit drugs are producing the delirium, then auditory hallucinations might also be present. Delirium is often directly attributable to drugs, alcohol or suicidal ingestion of some poison such as an overdose of aspirin or over-the-counter sleeping-pills, etc. Delirium occurs from many medical causes, from infection with or without fever to direct head injury. LSD sometimes causes delirium, as do any other illicit drugs of that type or amphetamines. Early poisoning with barbiturates or heroin can cause disorientation and memory defects. As mentioned before, schizophrenia itself can resemble a delirium. At any rate, the important thing is, if you have a patient with signs of delirium, you must ascertain if there are immediate causes for it such as head injury or drug ingestion, and refer the patient to an M.D. *immediately*.

Dementia (literally, lack of mind) is what we commonly think of as senility. There can be many causes of it. If the patient has a heart condition, his heart may not be pumping enough blood to his brain and may be responsible for the OBS you find on examination. Diabetes, for many reasons, can also be responsible for this condition, as can syphilis, kidney disorders, too few or too many salts in the blood, hardening of the arteries supplying the brain and thus decreasing the blood supply, etc. Your job is to find the signs of the progressive cognitive, emotional, and intellectual deficit as has been described. It is difficult sometimes to pick these up in conversation. Towards the end of an interview, if I have reason to suspect organic impairment, and *even if I don't* have reason to suspect OBS, I tell the patient that I would like to test his memory and play a few mental games with him, no matter how silly the questions may seem. I then proceed to ask him several of the memory and orientation questions outlined in Chapter 7.

There are specific memory defects or other organic signs which go along with alcoholic brain disease. These will be described in the chapter on alcoholism, Chapter 13.

## CASE VIGNETTES OF PATIENT'S PAST DRUG ABUSE

I have had several patients who complained of specific difficulty with memory or concentration lasting years after the prolonged heavy ingestion of LSD, amphetamines or other drugs. I have had these patients tested, and the psychological tests could not pickup these so-called memory deficits. The patients describe it as "not being able to remember as fast as I used to be able to remember," "having difficulty remembering the common names for objects but being able to ultimately do so," and other subjective, internal ideas that one's brain is not quite what it used to be. It is very difficult to separate the psychological reactions to heavy drug use and the possible but extremely subtle changes of mentation about which these patients complain. I have no doubt that, despite our inability to test these deficits with the finest psychological tools available, these changes in internal mental workings have taken place within the patient and that he responds to them. These untestable and undemonstrable "organic" complaints, however, cannot presently be labeled as organic brain syndrome, although I fully expect that this will occur in the near future, as we further refine our psychological testing tools.

# CHAPTER VI

# *Is Your Patient Psychotic Due to Medical Disease?*

The DSM III definition of psychosis is the presence of either hallucinations or delusions, incoherence, loose associations, marked poverty of thought, marked illogicality or behavior which is grossly disorganized or catatonic. To that I would add that persons with organic brain syndromes can have such poor judgment that their behavior can be termed psychotic. (This is probably subsumed under the term "disorganized," but I wanted to make it more explicit.) Similarly, severe depression leads to poverty of thought and severe mania leads to disorganization. In other words, people with affective disorder, schizophrenia or organic brain syndrome can be psychotic or not, depending on the presence of such symptoms.

In this chapter we will be concentrating on psychoses that have an origin in medical disease of which you can get hints if you ask the right questions.

It is important to note that the majority of the psychoses discussed in this chapter are also associated with an organic brain syndrome. Whenever you feel a patient is psychotic and the patient has signs of organic brain syndrome as well, he must be seen by a psychiatrist or internist before embarking on psychotherapy. It is advisable to remember, however, that acute schizophrenia can often be associated with confusion, clouded consciousness, disorientation, and memory or concentration defects, and can therefore resemble an organic brain syndrome. It is precisely because this is true that at some point an M.D. should interview the patient so as to avoid treating hyperthyroidism with psychosis as schizophrenia, for example.

A good history can begin the differentiation between medical diseases causing the psychosis and the so-called functional psychoses, if you ask the right questions and do a good mental status examination (see Chapter 7). Probably the first question that should be asked upon initial contact with a psychotic patient should be, "What drugs or alcohol have you been consuming?"

There are several syndromes of psychosis associated with alcohol; these are covered in the chapter on alcohol (Chapter 13). It is common knowledge that LSD, mescaline, amphetamines, barbiturates, or other illicit drugs, including marijuana, can cause psychosis which is difficult to differentiate from schizophrenia on occasion. Most of these "toxic" psychoses are associated with the signs of acute organic brain syndrome (delirium) which were presented in Chapter 5, whereas as often as not an acute schizophrenic can still be oriented to time, place, and person and may even be able to do serial sevens (see Chapter 7).

A word here about the symptoms of psychosis. Visual hallucinations are more common in "organic" psychosis than are auditory hallucinations. This is quite important to remember. If a patient complains primarily of visual hallucinations one should be quite suspicious of organic psychosis. Although this is less true if the visual hallucinations are accompanied by auditory ones, it is still a cue to "think organic."

There are "normal" hallucinations called "hypnagogic hallucinations," which occur to some persons just before they fall asleep. These are not considered psychotic if the rest of the mental status is clear. Particularly in older age groups, however, confusion, disorientation and possibly hallucinations occur towards evening and/or at bedtime. This is characteristic of the onset of senile brain disease, more rightly entitled senile organic brain syndrome or senile dementia, and learning from the history of these symptoms should stimulate suspicion. Note that the hallucinations, if present, are usually visual and are almost always associated with confusion, memory impairment, and disorientation occurring in late evening and usually clearing by morning or early in the day. Often these symptoms can be managed by *small doses* of phenothiazines in late afternoon, and by that approach, hospitalization may possibly be avoided. It is also noteworthy that *large doses* of phenothiazines might make organic impairment worse. Small doses of phenothiazines are equivalent to 50 mg. or less of chlorpromazine (Thorazine) per day (see Chapter 8).

The symptoms of senile OBS as just described can be caused by anything which prevents blood from reaching the brain. This is generally called cerebral ischemia. As a result, loss of neurons or impairment of their transmission of impulses can occur. This can be due to cardiac conditions or general arteriosclerosis (hardening of the arteries) of the brain, or of the smaller arteries and capillaries within the brain. *Whenever you find psychosis for the first time* in a patient over 50, "think organic." Very often, patients close to or over 50 will be depressed as well as psychotic since that is often the age of onset for major depressive disorder and involutional melancholia. It is therefore imperative that you do a good mental status examination with all patients in older age groups (this does not mean that younger patients should be slighted).

## CUSHINGS SYNDROME

Once in a while you may come across a person with this disease who is psychotic. Visual inspection of the patient is the best guide in this case. Cushings Syndrome is a disease of the adrenal glands in which those glands produce too much cortisone. *The same symptoms can occur if your patient is taking cortisone for some other ailment.*

The patient is usually fat, with a heavy round face which is often excessively red. There may be profound depression associated with psychosis, but mania is known to occur as well. Women tend to get more hair on their faces and abdomens. You can ask the patient if she has noticed increased facial hair, increased weight, and a tendency to drink a lot of water as well as urinate excessively. Frank diabetes is often also associated with this disease in which there is increased appetite as well as increased thirst. Frequently these symptoms occur in another disease of the adrenal glands, adreno-genital syndrome. The really important thing to remember is to LOOK at the patient and be suspicious if there is psychosis in a woman whose periods have stopped or become irregular, or in a man who recently developed a large paunch and is *heavy,* especially on his (or her) upper back. The thickening of the fat pads on the nape of the neck and between the shoulder blades is the so-called "buffalo hump" which is characteristic of this disease. As noted, this can occur from cortisone pills being taken for some other disorder. It cannot be overemphasized, therefore, that a good medication history should be obtained from the patient.

## HYPERTHYROIDISM (OVERACTIVITY OF THE THYROID GLAND)

Interestingly, hyperthyroidism (whose anxiety attack-like symptoms where described in Chapter 1) is often associated with severe depression and/or psychosis. It is very important to distinguish this psychosis or depression from psychological or so-called functional psychoses, because it is entirely reversible with proper thyroid medications.

The patient will seem exceptionally nervous, sweating, subjectively complain of being too warm; he will also have a rapid heart rate or complain of palpitations; he may complain of insomnia. He will have lost weight even in the face of increased appetite. The crucial question to be asked is, "Have you lost or gained weight, and how is your appetite?" Unfortunately, the most careful questioning will not differentiate hyperthyroidism from other,nonmedically caused psychoses. The important thing is to be suspicious and OBSERVE the patient for signs like "bulging eyes," enlargement of the base of the neck in front, tremors, etc., and *ask* about excessive anxiety, sweating, palpitations, insomnia, etc.

Sometimes hyperthyroidism can resemble schizophrenia so that questions about eating, sleeping, and tremulousness are very important, although they can not make the differentiation for you. The only sure way is to tell the supervising M.D. that hyperthyroidism is suspected and that he should order the proper laboratory blood tests.

It is important to recall that *this* psychosis may often be, but also may not be, associated with organic symptoms such as memory impairment, disorientation, and confusion.

## HYPOTHYROIDISM

As noted in the preceding pages, diseases of the thyroid are prominent among causes of several psychiatric syndromes. It would probably be ideal for every patient who comes to a psychotherapist to have a battery of blood tests, including those for thyroid disease. Since this is not possible, clinical observations and suspicions will determine who is selected to have such tests.

Patients with hypothyroidism (underactivity of the thyroid gland) also develop psychoses with hallucinations and delusions, and these are usually associated with signs of organic brain syndrome like memory defects. The patient may complain of, or you may notice, slowness of thought processes, depression, irritability, intolerance to cold, and general mental dullness or apathy. Depression and paranoid symptoms are commonly observed, but the personality structure of the person before the onset of the disease (premorbid personality structure) for the most part determines the symptoms within the psychosis.

A patient with hypothyroidism was described earlier in the text. It will be recalled that patients with this disease have usually gained considerable amounts of weight depending on how long the hypothyroidism has been present. The voice may be unusually low if female, or it may have become lower if male, or the patient may tell you that he has been hoarse for a few months and blame it on cigarettes. Hair may have become coarse and dry, and the patient may have lost some hair on his or her eyebrows, legs and abdomen or public region. Again, careful observation and questioning are what will prevent this patient from being treated for major depressive disorder instead of hypothyroidism.

## VITAMIN DEFICIENCIES OR EXCESSES

Deficiencies in vitamins, particularly of the B variety, can also be causes for organic brain syndrome with psychosis. Excess of vitamin D is another possible cause for psychosis, usually associated with OBS. The mechanisms by which vitamin deficiencies and excesses can cause psychosis with or without OBS are very complex. The important thing to remember is to ask the patient about his dietary habits and vitamin intake. The list of possible medical diseases causing psychosis is very extensive and the preceding paragraphs list but a few examples. It would be ideal if all psychotic patients, with or without OBS, could have a complete medical and neurological workup.

## NEUROLOGICAL DISEASES

In general, organic and psychological symptoms are frequent accompaniments to neurologic disease. Often the first sign of a brain tumor or minor stroke is a not easily definable "change in personality," most often noticed by relatives of the patient. A "simple" symptom such as fatigability can very occasionally herald myasthenia gravis. Euphoria is well known in acute multiple sclerosis, but depression and irritability are also common. Interestingly, in multiple sclerosis lability of affect with some involuntary crying or laughter occurs, but only after neurologic symptoms have emerged. It is not our purpose here to go into all neurologic diseases, but rather to point out the large overlap in symptomatology between neurologic and psychiatric diseases.

In general, when neurologic illnesses are associated with psychosis they are also associated with signs of organic brain syndrome. Sometimes psychotic patients exhibit signs of apparent neurologic disease, especially when they show organic symptoms. I have had several patients who had severe depression almost to the point where they couldn't talk. They complained of poor memory, and indeed had very poor recent memory, to which their families attested. One of them had tremors as well, and we were sure he had an undisclosed neurological illness. None was discovered, but on gross mental status testing all tests were deficient in some aspects, most generally associated with intellectual functioning. Complete neurologic workups, including arterial visualization in some, revealed no demonstrable neurologic problems. Then, and only then, when the neurologic workups were complete, we started him on antidepressants. As the depression lifted, so did the "organicity," until, when the depression was gone, so were all the signs of organic brain syndrome, and, incidentally, tremors. On the other hand, I had one patient with severe Parkinson's disease, whose tremors got progressively worse, and who, although he didn't complain of depression, had all the psychomotor and vegetative signs of depression. Treatment of his depression with ECT resulted in a very significant decrease in the neurologic signs of his Parkinson's Disease. Improvement in Parkinsonian symptoms following ECT treatment of depression has also been reported in the literature. (Lebensohn and Jenkins, 1975).

# CHAPTER VII

# *Outline Guide for First Interview*

The circumstances surrounding the initial interview will determine its length and, hence, to what extent you will want to get all the information cited below in one session. For example, the patient's state of mind, to a certain extent, determines how long an interview he can tolerate, as well as what information you need. Other factors affecting this information-gathering are: 1) whether you are or someone else is going to be the patient's primary therapist; 2) whether the patient is *in* the hospital, or, this interview might determine if the patient needs hospitalization; 3) what your functional role is with the patient; 4) who is supervising you on the case or the interview, if anyone.

There are basically three main objectives in the first interview. The first is to ascertain the person's *"chief complaint,"* that is, the reason the patient gives for being at the interview. As the person talks and the *history* of the *chief complaint* becomes known, the next task is to arrive at a tentative working diagnosis, even if it's "probably neurotic" or "probably psychotic." The third objective is to then decide what you are going to do about the situation, i.e., formulate a tentative working treatment plan. Sometimes all you have time for in this first session is to obtain the chief complaint and the history of the chief complaint, without being able to ask all the other important questions which are covered below. There are certain questions which really *must* be covered and others which can be asked at a future time.

The first important thing is that you conceptualize the PATIENT'S view of why he came to see you. No matter how sophisticated your insight into his "real" problem may be, you might not want to immediately tell a patient who came to you under pressure from his spouse that the only thing that will save the marriage is five-times-a-week psychoanalysis. On the other hand, a psychotic patient who came under pressure from his family, and says he doesn't think there is anything wrong with him, can be told that you think that he has problems in certain areas (name them) and that he can be helped by both medication and psychotherapy if he is willing to give them a chance (either in or out of the hospital, based on other factors defined below).

Remember, for the first interview you have three major tasks and *that's all*: Ascertain the chief complaint, decide on a working diagnosis, and formulate what you are going to do about it. Don't let yourself get sidetracked by the patient into talking about his childhood, etc., and thus lose time during which you could be finding out about medical or biological signs which point to important diagnostic categories. If you are going to see the patient again you can talk about his childhood some other time; if you are *not* going to see him again, the discussion is irrelevant. Intrinsically there is *nothing* in this interview which precludes psychoanalytic therapy once the desirability of it is established and medication-responsive syndromes are ruled out. The outline below is useful to have in mind as you interview the patient. It really contains the bare essentials that are necessary to achieving the three objectives stated above.

## CHIEF COMPLAINT AND HISTORY OF CHIEF COMPLAINT

1. What is "chief complaint"?
2. *When* did "chief complaint" start?
3. *Why* did patient choose *this* day to seek help?
4. Did "chief complaint" ever occur in past, and if so, what set it off?
5. MEDICATIONS, SELF-MEDICATIONS, past and present; don't forget BIRTH CONTROL PILLS.
6. DRUG USE OR ABUSE, past and present. Ask about: Hallucinations with or without drugs or alcohol.
7. ALCOHOL USE OR ABUSE, past or present. Ask about: Hallucinations with or without alcohol.
8. MEDICAL ILLNESSES PAST AND PRESENT, injuries, operations.
9. LOST OR GAINED WEIGHT during this *present* "chief complaint" or illness—how is appetite and taste of food?
10. How is patient *sleeping* these nights? How many hours? Does he wake up early, wake up intermittently, have difficulty falling asleep or not sleep, does he sleep during the day?
11. WHATEVER the chief complaint is, *always* ask patient if he has ever attempted suicide or has been thinking about it lately.
12. Ask about *Unusual Perceptual Phenomena.*

*Type Question:* Have you ever experienced unsual things like hearing noises or voices that really weren't there? (Check both for psychosis and anything from a middle ear infection to a brain tumor.) *Visual Hallucinations* in the *absence of any other signs* of psychosis or alcoholism should alert you to the possibility of organic brain impairment (diabetes, ischemia, tumor, etc.)

*Type Question:* Have you ever had spots before your eyes or seen lights flashing when there were no real lights flashing? Have you ever had visions of people or animals?

*Type Question* for other sensory phenomena: Have you ever *smelled* something funny that the people you were with didn't smell? (This question is particularly important to ask of persons who have violent outbursts of rage or rampages of impulsive behavior which lasts from minutes to hours. If validated by EEG, these patients are said to have "uncinate fits" or temporal lobe epilepsy.) The nerves from the olfactory (smell) endings have connections in the temporal lobe and often people with this type of epilepsy smell "something burning" or give some other description just before the attack occurs. Olfactory hallucinations also occur in schizophrenia.

If at this point you are out of time or the patient is emotionally fatigued, the following questions should be asked the next session. THESE QUESTIONS ARE ESSENTIAL and should be asked soon after beginning hospitalization or outpatient therapy since, as will be noted below, they are screening questions for various physical diseases which can mascarade as anything from schizophrenia to anxiety neurosis.

1. *Change in Physical Appearance; Hair Distribution or Quantity.* Enlargement of hat size, jaw, shoe size or glove size can point to acromegaly—a disorder of the pituitary gland. Changes in hair distribution can point to many things: loss of hair on legs and eyebrows—thyroid; increased abdominal hair and change in its pattern in females—adrenals, ovaries, pituitary, thyroid; loss of chest hair, facial hair in males—testicles, adrenals, pituitary.

2. *Change in Voice: Males 12–16 Normal Deepening.* Either sex's voice deepening after puberty could indicate thyroid problems, various neurological disorders such as myasthenia gravis, or lung cancer in smokers. Incidently lung cancers are notorious for producing all kinds of chemicals and syndromes including psychosis.

3. *Change in Menstrual Regularity.* A host of things affect menstruation. It should be noted that phenothiazines, depression, tricyclics, anorexia nervosa, schizophrenia, and many other drugs and syndromes can be associated with complete cessation of menstruation. Mental state during pregnancy? The answer to this question may indicate whether presently used birth control pills are partly responsible for present condition.

4. *Head injury or Seizure.* Self-explanatory.

5. *Fainting or Blackouts.* Check for anemia, hypoglycemia, hysteria, hyperventilation, orthostatic hypotension, petit mal epilepsy, alcoholism and many other causes for brain impairment.

6. *Is Patient a Food-Faddist or Vitamin Taker?* People on high protein, low calorie diets who eat fish in excess of what the programs recommend, or other fish-eaters, have occasionally been found to have mercury poisoning in the United States (many more in Japan and other countries whose main source of animal protein is fish), which presents itself as nervousness, irritability, etc., and can be confused with neurotic symptoms. Vitamin faddists can get vitamin poisoning—particularly vitamins A and D both of which can present psychiatrically.

7. *Memory and Concentration.* These can be disrupted both by psychological disease and organic brain disease and are crucial in diagnosing organic brain disease. It is common for acute schizophrenics to be unable to perform the memory and concentration tests on the mental status examination. However, when they are calmed and improved some weeks later, they are quite able to do so. Persons with permanent organic brain impairment with psychosis may be "cured" of their psychosis, but they remain unable to recall what they had for dinner the night before, etc. on the mental status examination.

## FORMAL MENTAL STATUS

1. *Orientation Tests*

(a) Time: what is today's date; month, day, year?

(b) Place: what is the name of this place; what place did you come from?

(c) Person: who am *I*? (Don't ask the patient who *he* is unless you suspect hysterical (fake) amnesia; no matter how "organic" somebody gets, they *almost never* forget their name;

hysterics, however, *will* sometimes deny that they remember their names.) The patient may not be able to recall your name but should be able to say that you are the nurse, the doctor, the social worker, etc.

1. Have we ever met before? (This checks for confabulation, a specific defect in which the patient, being aware of "holes" in his memory attempts to fill in the gaps with stories he is not quite sure did not happen. Confabulation is seen in alcoholic brain damage more often than in senile or other organicities.)

2. *Memory Tests.* (a) Recent Memory: What did you have for your most recent meal?; What did you have for the meal before that?

1. I am going to tell you three unrelated words; I want you to try to remember them. I will ask you what they are later. Tennis, cereal, blue, repeat once and have the patient repeat them (also tests concentration).

(b) Remote Memory and Concentration—Serial 7's: Tell the patient to subtract 7 from 100 then 7 from that and 7 from that, continue even if they are doing it totally wrong, until you have decided, based on either their intellectual or educational level or their organic brain impairment that they are incapable of doing this (or capable of it).

With patients whom I presume to be well educated, I often tell them that I wish to check their memory, and I ask them if they remember their algebra. I then ask them a simple equation in algebra and if they can answer it I presume this particular part of the mental status examination to be okay. If they can't do the algebra I proceed to 100 minus 17 and 98 plus 19, and then finally to 100 minus 7. This way of proceeding tests educational level and memory function and can give many valuable clues.

(c) Who is the President of the United States now? Who was the President before him? and before him? Most organically *un*impaired people can name the presidents backwards in sequence for about five presidents if they are old enough, or have completed high school. Uneducated or very unintelligent people may only be able to name two.

Organically impaired persons may recall those 30 years previous, but be unable to name recent ones.

3. *Proverbs.* Although this is part of the "mental status" examination it is highly debated as to *what* if anything, proverb testing measures. Supposedly, if the person answers in certain ways it may be either self-referential or indicative of "concreteness," which allegedly occurs more often in schizophrenia and in some organic brain syndromes. Examples will follow. Proverbs may not be too useful diagnostically if the patient has never heard them before or was not brought up in this country. It can be argued that adults of normal intelligence should be able to get the abstract meaning of the proverb even if they never heard it before. However, *in the presence of an otherwise clear mental status,* I personally would draw no conclusions if the patient could not abstract the proverbs.

Ask the patient what does this proverb mean? Have you ever heard it before?

1. People who live in glass houses shouldn't throw stones. The standard answers to this should include the idea of either those who are equally guilty shouldn't point fingers at others or those who are equally vulnerable or open to criticism shouldn't criticize others.

The "concrete" answer classically is "because they'll break the windows" followed by an *inability* to give the other (more abstract) meanings.

2. A stitch in time saves nine. Standard answer includes concept of catching trouble early, or doing some task before it gets too big or out of hand. I had a schizophrenic patient who said "well, if I sew it up I only use nine stitches and I save time. I saved nine dollars by stitching nine times." This is, you will admit, both concrete *(not abstract)* and self-referential, besides not making too much sense.

You can use any proverbs you know and that the patient says he has heard before. You can even ask if the person remembers whether they *ever* knew what the proverb meant. Inability to abstract on proverbs however, by *itself,* is *not diagnostic* of anything.

## BACK TO RECENT MEMORY AND CONCENTRATION

Do you recall the three words I told you to memorize? What were they? Tennis, cereal, and blue.

It is not necessary to ask the above questions like a Gestapo agent; they can be interspersed into the conversation between you and the patient. Here is an example of how it can be done.

T = Therapist, P = Patient.

T: "What made you come here today?"

P: "My nerves have been getting progressively worse."

T: "Since when?"

P: "Well, my mother died three years ago and I haven't been the same since. I've been nervous and irritable and depressed."

T: (Checking for family history of suicide) "What did your mother die of?"

P: "Chirrhosis of the liver and pancreatitis."

T: "Oh, was she an alcoholic?" (T's thoughts—probable family history of depression since most alcoholics, especially female alcoholics are chronically depressed.)

P: "Yes, she was an alcoholic and I never had a father. She made my nerves worse when she was alive. She made my father's nerves bad too, which is probably why he divorced her. I was only three when they separated. She was drinking heavily even at that time."

T: "What do you mean when you say your nerves are bad?"

P: "I've been hearing strange things like people knocking on doors, but I go to the door and there's no one there . . . And I can't concentrate and I think I'm losing my memory. I can't remember the simplest things."

T: "Have you been using any drugs?" (note signs of possible organic brain disorder—memory defects, concentration, irritability).

P: "I used to use a lot of 'speed' when I was depressed in the past, but I haven't used anything except 'pot' lately."

T: "When was the last time you used 'speed'?"

P: "Oh about two months ago, I've been trying to diet."

T: "How long have you been depressed?"

P: "I've been depressed for three years since my mother died."

T: "Did your mother's death make you depressed?" (NEVER ASSUME!)

P: "I got depressed before her death actually because she was sick and she leaned on me a lot. My mother was really terrible—even when I was a child. She was always drunk, she beat me a lot, she never let me have boyfriends. When she got really sick from the alcoholism she wanted me to take total care of her. That's when I started to get depressed."

T: "Did you ever get depressed before that?" (Be wary of getting sidetracked about childhood.)

P: "I've been depressed my whole life it seems, but actually sometimes I'm normal, in fact sometimes I'm hyperactive."

T: "What do you mean by hyperactive?"

P: "Well, I clean the house, move furniture around, get interested in going back to school again, get interested in all kinds of projects."

T: "Do you get interested or do you actually do all kinds of projects?"

P: "I actually do some projects, especially those that I can finish fast. I do others when I'm really high."

T: "Too high or just normally feeling good?"

P: "No, too high."

T: "What do you mean by too high?"

P: "Well, I'm feeling so good that I make everyone laugh around me. My thoughts speed up and I can't concentrate—and that's off 'speed.'"

P: "I don't like to sleep when I'm high either. I only get about four hours and that's enough. Sleeping seems like a waste of time when I feel that way."

T: "How are you sleeping now?"

P: "I can't sleep at night at all; every time I lie down I just think bad thoughts. I can't remember anything good about my mother, only the bad things, that's what I mean about my memory going bad."

T: "Are you sleeping during the day?"

P: "Yes, that's all I do is sleep and eat. I've gained 40 pounds in three years. I took off 10, but I'm still 30 pounds overweight."

T: "So you generally gain weight when you're depressed? What is it like when you're high?"

P: "I always go on a diet when I'm high?"

T: "Do you lose weight?"

P: "Oh yes, I'm much fatter now than I usually am."

T: "How long do the highs last and how long do the downs last?"

P: "A few weeks for the highs and a few years for the downs."

T: "Have you ever tried to kill yourself?"

P: "I tried three times. Twice I took overdoses but I got scared and realized I really didn't want to die so I vomited up the pills. Last year I slit my wrist."

T: "Did you need stitches?"

P: "It was just a scratch, no stitches."

T: "So you get depressed enough to want to die but then you really don't want to."

P: "I was drunk both times I took the overdoses."

T: "Do you drink when you're depressed?"

P: "I drink about one drink and I'm drunk and angry and depressed and I black out and can't remember anything afterwards—I don't even remember taking the drink."

T: "Do you ever black out when you're not drinking?"

P: "No."

T: "You said you've tried to kill yourself in the past; have you thought about doing it recently?"

P: "I've thought about it but I'm not going to do it."

T: "Why not?"

P: "I can only get the courage when I'm drunk and my husband doesn't let me get drunk anymore."

T: "I'd like to get back to the 'knocks at the door'. Have your ever heard other things like clicks or actual voices when people were not around?"

P: "I heard like bells but I knew they weren't really there."

T: "Aside from blacking out after one drink, have you ever been unconscious or had a head injury?"

P: "I fell off a horse when I was about 10 years old and my mother said I was unconscious for a few minutes but I don't remember anything about it."

T: "I'd like to go back to the original problem for a while. What made you come here *today* specifically?"

P: "Well, I just couldn't take it anymore; my nerves were driving me crazy. I want to get my head together . . . I am so nervous all the time and I'm horribly depressed."

T: "Have you taken any medicine for your nerves?"

P: "Yeah, the family doctor gave me little white tablets a long time ago, but I ran out of them about two months ago."

T: "You're not taking *anything* now—no medicines, no drugs, not anything?"

P: "Well not for the last two months anyway."

T: "How about birth control pills?"

P: "Oh, yes, of course I take those, but that's not medicine."

T: "Not in the usual sense, but birth control pills are depressing to some people. When did you start taking them?"

P: "About two years ago."

T: "You've been depressed for three years and off and on before that; did you ever see a psychiatrist for it?"

P: "Before my mother died she wouldn't let me, and since she died I figured I was just still mourning and no one could help me. My husband has been trying to help but he just makes me feel worse because I can't do the things a wife is supposed to do, so he does them and then I feel guilty. I can't even go to bed with him."

This merely an excerpt from an interview, and obviously many things are not covered, particularly psychological issues around this patient's mother's death, and further probing about why the patient came that particular day—which may be because of her husband, another area which is not presented in the excerpt. What can be gleaned from this part of the interview is the patient's chief complaint, its partial history, her sleeping and eating habits, drug and alcohol usage, one important piece of family history, a smattering of checking for unusual perceptual phenomena and the recognition of what is *left out,* providing a concept of what *should be included* is kept in mind. One very important part of this interview which is not included is the formal mental status examination. This is particularly important since this woman was complaining of vaguely organic symptomatology. The mental status examination in this woman turned out to be normal. It was introduced to her by saying, "I want to check your memory and concentration. Some of the things I ask you will seem silly, but please go along with me anyway." Every therapist has his or her own way of introducing this vital part of the interview.

Chief complaint, as stated by patient, "nerves getting bad" as perceived by the therapist and patient (ultimately); depression three or more years duration.

## DIAGNOSTIC POSSIBILITIES

1. a) Cyclothymic personality with hysterical features.

b) The possibility of manic-depressive illness should be kept in mind but needs more supporting evidence such as distinct phases obvious to husband and clearer definition of highs without the probable use of amphetamines.

2. Amphetamine-induced depression with incipient psychosis. Note: patient denies recent amphetamine abuse, but this should still be a consideration.

3. Possible pathological intoxication. (Pathological intoxication is the occurrence of hostile, violent or impulsive behavior, with intoxication, blackouts and memory loss for the period of time following one or at the most two normal size alcohol-containing drinks.) This patient attempted suicide twice after having one cocktail, which can be considered impulsive since she immediately aborted her own attempts.

## TENTATIVE TREATMENT PLAN

1. Possibly hospitalize unless extreme objections from husband, for, despite denial, patient is probably suicidal

although she is not likely to attempt suicide while sober. Possibly exists, however, that she will deliberately drink, knowing that she is likely to attempt suicide again.

Here again, without additional commentary, is the outline for the first interview. Ascertain as much of the following information as possible.

## CHIEF COMPLAINT—WHAT IS IT?

1. When did it start.
2. Why did patient choose *this* day to seek help.
3. History of chief complaint

(a) Has it occurred in past; if yes, when, how long did it last, what set it off, was it treated, if so, by whom or what and did treatment work.

4. What medicines or drugs is patient now using and has patient used for similar discomfort in past.
5. Drug abuse, particularly amphetamines and barbiturates and alcohol—in *all* age groups; younger patients should be asked about hallucinogens, marijuana, hashish, cocaine, etc.
6. Relevant medical illnesses, operations or injuries.
7. Biological Signs

*Sleep disorders:* waking up much too early; inability to fall asleep; persistent intermittent awakening; too much sleep; inability to get out of bed (more than ten hours sleep); sleep during day; not sleeping at night.

*Appetite disorders:* eating excessively; being excessively *hungry* but *eating normally* for fear of gaining weight; loss of appetite; food being tasteless; WEIGHT GAIN or LOSS.

*Psychomotor symptoms: observe* foot tapping, hand wringing or fist clenching; facial expression; *rate* of speech; use or nonuse of hands in talking; unusual body posture; static body position, restlessness.

8. Suicide potential *presently* as well as past attempts.

## ADDITIONAL DIAGNOSTIC QUESTIONS NECESSARY TO TENTATIVE WORKING DIAGNOSIS:

1. unusual perceptual phenomena and hallucinations.
2. changes in physical appearance,
   especially: loss of hair on legs, eyebrows; pubic region, thinning of head-hair, excessive hair anywhere; enlargement of base of neck in front or in back; drooping of one eyelid or one corner of mouth.
3. changes of voice; slurring of speech.
4. changes in *memory, concentration.*
5. regularity of menstruation; mental state during pregnancies.
6. Sexual enjoyment.
7. head injury or seizure (convulsion).
8. fainting, blackouts.
9. concern for physical health; vitamin taking.
10. FORMAL MENTAL STATUS EXAMINATION especially indicated where difficulties in memory and concentration are in question.

Should you feel it necessary in order to set up your personal style with the patient, nothing prevents you from indicating that this style of questioning and interacting is really only for the first or second interview and that future sessions will more than likely be rather different.

# CHAPTER VIII

# *Minor Tranquilizers*

I presume that minor tranquilizers are called minor to distinguish them from those major tranquilizers phenothiazines and phenothiazine-like drugs—which are used in more major or serious disorders. However, anybody who has ever taken one of the minor tranquilizers knows that its effect can be major, indeed. Furthermore, they are addicting—that is, not minor. At any rate, they are used primarily for anxiety and I use them for anxiety-dpression where anxiety is primary. They have wide application outside of their use for mental disorders, as they are very effective muscle relaxants, and as well are used for anxiety where it contributes or results from a wide variety of medical disorders.

The minor tranquilizers discussed here are:

| | |
|---|---|
| Librium | (chlordiazepoxide) |
| Valium | (diazepam) |
| Serax | (oxazepam) |
| Ativan | (lorazepam) |
| Verstran | (prazepam) |
| Tranxene | (chlorazepate) |
| Meprotabs | (Meprobamate) |
| Equanil | (Meprobamate) |
| Meprospan | (Meprobamate) |
| Miltown | (Meprobamate) |
| Vistaril | (hydroxyzine) |
| Solacen | (tybamate) |

All the drugs listed have been found to be consistently better than placebo in reducing anxiety. That's because Valium, Tranxene and Verstran all become the same active metabolite, as soon as they are administered, and Librium has as a minor active metabolite, the same metabolite as the others (desmethyldiazepam). Valium, Tranxene and Verstran, then, are virtually identical. In practice Ativan, Serax, Valium and the others are all virtually identical in their ability to decrease anxiety and panic states. I suppose they are being made for two reasons: 1) free enterprise and 2) to allow the M.D. to give a "new" pill to patients. Equanil and the others are identical, and equal to the others in decreasing anxiety. Other drugs, like Librax, have Librium combined with antispasmodic agents for the stomach, and Miltrate has an antiangina drug in it. Dalmane is a sleeping pill derived closely from Valium-type chemicals. In this chapter we will consider simply the minor tranquilizers as listed above and not deal with combination products or derivatives.

In talking about the minor tranquilizers it is necessary to immediately begin talking about dosage. In doses of less than 20 mg. per day of Librium many studies show Librium equal to placebo (Klein and Davis, 1969). However, in *most* studies on neurotic anxiety, all the drugs listed and barbiturates in sedative doses were better than placebo when used in high enough dosage. Most studies showed that the effects of any of the tranquilizers listed above was equal to the effects of any other, if given in pharmacologically equivalent doses to neurotic, anxious patients with or without other symptoms such as depression or phobia. The majority of studies indicated that the minor tranquilizers were not as good as phenothiazines at relieving anxiety when used alone in major psychiatric illnesses such as schizophrenia.

Although I have heard noises (but no proof) that benzodiazepines may possess some antipsychotic activity, and there is recent evidence (Baestrup and Squires, Brit. J. Psychiatry 1978) that there is a benzodiazepine receptor in the brain which pressures the search for an endogenous minor tranquilizer of the benzodiazepine class. If there was one, we could all say that our endogenous benzodiazepine supply was down and we wouldn't have any qualms—as many people do—about taking an exogenous supply

As with any tranquilizer, including the major tranquilizers, the drugs under discussion can be depressing. Here, clinical judgment is very important. Anxiety itself is depressing and is often difficult to separate from depression clinically. In attempting to assess how depressed the patient is, versus how much his anxiety plays a role in his depression, I usually use biological criteria. If the patient has a sleep disorder such as early morning awakening, a loss of appetite or heavily increased appetite or other biological signs mentioned in the chapter on depression, I usually assume the depression to be primary, and I treat it with antidepressants. If, however, no biological signs of depression are present, but the patient complains of depression and anxiety, I usually assume the anxiety to be primary and treat it with minor tranquilizers. Often a combination of antidepressants (tricyclic type) and minor tranquilizers is useful even when no biological signs of depression exist. However, as already noted, depressions without the biological signs are less likely to respond to the antidepressants. It is important to realize that minor depression, without biological signs, will probably respond most favorably to psychotherapy alone or psychotherapy combined with minor tranquilizers if the anxiety component is strong. Often, when anxiety is relieved the patient feels less depressed despite the fact that the tranquilizers can be psychologically depressing.

The minor tranquilizers are *not* placebo. They work, and work well, at relieving anxiety, tension, and associated mild depression, apathy, etc. which often result from anxiety.

The *major problem* with the *minor tranquilizers* is that they can be *physically addicting*. They are not really addicting in low doses but can be seriously addicting in high doses. They also show the typical course of any addicting drug which begins with tolerance. That is, the original dose of the drug no longer gives the *original anti-anxiety response;* more drug is needed to obtain the same response. It is important, therefore, to keep checking with the patient about the quantity of tranquilizer he is taking. There is a strong tendency to increase the dosage once the patient has found that the drug alleviates his symptoms. Doses of Librium or Valium in excess of 40 mg. per day are probably addictive and should not be withdrawn abruptly. Doses of Meprobamate above four capsules a day should be considered addictive and should not be withdrawn abruptly either.

The signs and symptoms of withdrawal from any of these drugs are similar to withdrawal of any central nervous system depressant. These signs are: excitability, nervousness, leg cramps and twitches, nausea and vomiting, and possibly convulsions *if* the addiction has existed for a long time and/or on a very high dose.

Interestingly enough, diazepam is now the drug of choice used by many physicians in the United States to stop epileptic seizures and prevent them in alcoholic withdrawal. It is a better choice than phenothiazines for seizure activity. As with any tranquilizer, major or minor, the effects of the drug are increased by, or are additive with, the effects of liquor, sleeping-pills, anesthetics, and other tranquilizers. Patients should be warned about drinking while on the minor tranquilizers since they will tend to get sleepy more easily on their usual amount of liquor.

## SIDE EFFECTS

There are extremely few consistent side effects from the minor tranquilizers. One has already been noted, namely, depression. Probably the most common side effect is drowsiness, which may wear off in three days if the dose is not too high. If drowsiness persists, the dose may have to be lowered. Other, very infrequent reactions such as "paradoxical excitement," panic or rage do occur.

All in all, however, the minor tranquilizers are excellent drugs for the treatment of neurotic anxiety or mixed anxiety and depression, as well as for anxiety and tension resulting from physical illness. They can be taken with almost all other drugs without harmful side effects. Caution should be exercised with liquor and sleeping pills. As with *any* drug, the possibility of deformed children should be kept in mind if the drugs are given during the first three months of pregnancy. There have been consistent reports that benzodiazepines and meprobamate (minor tranquilizers) have been associated with an increased risk of congenital malformations. It is always advisable to stop all medications, if possible, during pregnancy.

Often, I have seen schizophrenic patients who are taking major tranquilizers benefit from the addition of minor tranquilizers. This probably is due to the more antipsychotic properties of the phenothiazines as distinct from their antianxiety properties. The minor tranquilizers are specific antianxiety agents but have little or *no* antipsychotic properties that have been substantiated. In other words, minor tranquilizers are *not a substitute* for phenothiazines and should not be used as such. They *may* help further reduce anxiety in patients who also need antipsychotic drugs as well.

The minor tranquilizers can often be used to calm agitation in major depression as well. Unfortunately, however, this is not usually the case, and major tranquilizers are frequently needed in conjunction with tricyclic antidepressants. However, given the additive side effects of major tranquilizers and tricyclic antidepressants, it is worth a try to give the anxious depressed patient a fair trial on minor tranquilizers before going to the major ones.

A word about the use of minor tranquilizers in neurotic anxiety. It is a very critical decision to use minor tranquilizers in mild to moderate neurotic anxiety. There is certainly validity in the concept that if one chemically deprives the neurotic patient of the anxiety he is experiencing, he will be less likely to seek solutions to the conflicts which are presumably causing the anxiety. However—and this is why the decision is so crucial—anxiety in excess can itself interfere with psychotherapeutic work and the ability to deal effectively with interpretations.

In general, at least temporarily, minor tranquilizers are indicated if the person is dysfunctional in a major area of his life *as a result of neurotic anxiety*. Even this statement needs modification, however, because certainly phobias produce tremendous anxiety in the face of the phobic situation, yet reducing that anxiety will probably not reduce the phobia—even if the phobia is causing a major dysfunction. In short, minor tranquilizers do not always work. They reduce anxiety, not conflict. On the other hand, where neurotic anxiety is causing severe difficulty with work, relaxation, or interpersonal relations, minor tranquilizers can be of considerable benefit when used as a temporary measure.

# CHAPTER IX

# *Major Tranquilizers: Phenothiazines*

*Major Tranquilizers: Antipsychotic agents, Phenothiazines, Thioxanthines, Butyrophenones*

Phenothiazines were discovered in the mid-1950s and to a great extent are responsible for shortening the duration of hospital stay for many types of psychotic patients. Some of the more commonly used phenothiazines are:

| | |
|---|---|
| Thorazine (chlorpromazine) | Prolixin (fluphenazine) |
| Mellaril (thioridazine) | Permitil (fluphenazine) |
| Stelazine (trifluoperazine) | Trilafon (perphenazine) |
| Vesprin (trifluoperazine) | Compazine (prochlorperazine) |
| Serentil (mesoridazine) | Phenergan (promethazine) |
| Quide (piperacetazine) | Sparine (promazine) |
| | Tindal (acetophenazine) |

A more complete list is found in the Glossary of Drugs under Major Tranquilizers. The following drugs, although not phenothiazines, have similar actions against psychotic thinking and agitation and have similar side effects (in talking about phenothiazines these drugs are *understood to be included*):

| | |
|---|---|
| Haldol (haloperidol) | Taractan (chloroprothixene) |
| | Navane (thiothixene) |
| Serenace (haloperidol) | Solatran (chloroprothixene) |

Phenothiazines are also potent antiemetics (prevent nausea and vomiting) and some of them, like Compazine and Phenergan, are used more commonly for that purpose than for antipsychotic action.

Essentially, phenothiazines are used in treating psychotic thinking (thought disorganization and delusions) as well as hallucinatory experience and agitation. They can be and are sometimes used for severe neurotic anxiety states. They are used to control acute mania because the specific drug for mania, Lithium, takes about two weeks to exert its maximum antimanic effect, where phenothiazines act within hours if a high enough dose is given. Clearly, the phenothiazines are used in a wide variety of conditions, but mainly where there exists psychosis with or without agitation or severe agitation even if unaccompanied by psychosis. They were once used for alcoholic hallucinosis and "D.T.s" but diazepam (Valium) and chlordiazepoxide (Librium) have been found to be more advantageous for alcoholic states since they also help prevent withdrawal seizures.

The dosage of phenothiazines is extremely variable and does not depend solely on either the size or weight of the patient or his state of psychotic disorganization or agitation. This is important to realize because often, unconsciously, we tend to feel differently about patients who we know are on supposedly large doses of phenothiazines. We tend to think that the sicker the patient is the higher the dose of medication he needs. This may be true to a limited extent but, to give an example, older patients, even if they are floridly psychotic, require less antipsychotic than younger patients, primarily because of the rate of excretion. Does this mean that someone with a lower rate of excretion is *less* psychotic than someone who, because of a higher rate of excretion, takes more phenothiazine? Studies have reported (Klein and Davis, 1969) that chlorpromazine (Thorazine) in doses at or below 300 mg./day is equal to or slightly better than placebo *as often* as it is found to be more effective than placebo. However, when given at doses of 500 mg./day or more, it is always more effective than placebo. The list of dosages of other antipsychotic drugs which are equivalent to 100 mg. of chlopromazine is very extensive.

A short list of the dosages of phenothiazines equivalent to 100 mg. of Thorazine, using the most commonly prescribed phenothiazines, is:

| | |
|---|---|
| Stelazine 5 mg. | Trilafon 8 mg. |
| Prolixin 5 mg. | Haldol 2 mg. |
| Mellaril 100 mg. | Navane 5 mg. |

The antipsychotic dose per day of Stelazine is 20 mg., Prolixin 15 mg., Mellaril 400 mg. (300 mg. sometimes), Trilafon 24 mg., Haldol 8 mg. and Navane 15-20 mg. Unless the patient has had a trial for two weeks of an antipsychotic drug in that range, or unless his age or medical status (weight) preclude using the drug in that range, the patient has not had an adequate trial. Yes, people get better on lower dosages, but not always, and not if they are floridly psychotic or agitated. Furthermore, phenothiazines sometimes take up to two weeks to reduce specifically psychotic symptoms (as opposed to core schizophrenic symptoms), even if you give them in those dosage ranges.

## SIDE EFFECTS

Side effects are often dose-dependent, that is, reducing the dose may reduce the side effects. Allergic reactions such as jaundice (hepatitis), or skin reactions such as rashes or swelling, redness and itching upon exposure to sunlight are generally *not* dose-dependent and can even occur occasionally with one dose.

Generally, although not the prescriber of these drugs, you will usually be in a position to observe their side effects as well as their main effect. The main effects of phenothiazines and similar drugs are: 1) elimination of hallucinations; 2) decrease in delusional thinking; 3) decrease in agitation; 4) organization of thought processes and verbal productions; 5) decrease in anxiety. A comment here: The patient may still have delusions, but he no longer "cares" about them as much.

It is important to realize that improvement in these parameters is dependent on many factors, route of administration, for example. Agitation can be eliminated almost immediately by giving enough phenothiazine I.M. (injected into the muscle). This usually puts the patient to sleep temporarily, but the delusions and hallucinations will take much longer to disappear—around one to two weeks if the proper dose is administered over that period of time. Should the patient continue to hallucinate or be heavily delusional after two weeks on a particular dose, you should suggest to your medical back-up that the dose be increased.

The most commonly seen side effect is "sedation." The patient will complain of feeling sleepy. This is more common with certain types of phenothiazines than with others, but *all* can and *do* cause sedation. You can reassure the patient that the sleepiness is a side effect and will wear off in a week or so. If the patient still feels sleepy or "stoned" after 14 days on a drug, a decreased dose may be considered. This is also important to note after a patient has been on the same dose for six to eight months. If at that time he begins to feel sleepy, and it is *certain* that the sleepiness is phenothiazine-related, it may indicate that he is improving and also needs a slight decrease in dose.

You will often be asked if other preparations or drugs can be used safely with phenothiazines. In general, most over-the-counter preparations are safe with phenothiazines. The big caution is *alcohol,* which makes the person on phenothiazines very sleepy very quickly if he attempts to drink as much as he did without phenothiazines. Also, some over-the-counter cough medications contain narcotics or synthetic narcotic-like drugs which also add to the sedative properties of the phenothiazines. Naturally, sleeping pills of any type, nonprescription included, are additive with these drugs. In general, however, the phenothiazines are "safe" drugs to take with most other drugs. This is definitely opposite to the case of MAO inhibitors which will be discussed shortly.

The next most common side effects that patients complain of are dry mouth, stuffy nose and constipation, all of which are due to the anticholinergic properties of phenothiazines. These side effects generally persist as long as the drug is taken. I usually suggest that the patient chew sugarless* gum for the dry mouth and take an occasional tablespoon of milk of magnesia if the constipation gets too bad. Less commonly, patients on phenothiazines complain of blurred vision at close range. Sometimes a different phenothiazine is worth a try in this case, if it does as good a job as the original in checking the symptomatology which necessitated phenothiazines. Otherwise, a simple pair of over-the-counter magnifying glasses often alleviates the difficulty. If the dose is high enough (more than 200 mg. of chlorpromazine or the equivalent per day) almost every patient will experience orthostatic hypotension (ortho = change in; static = position; hypo = low; tension = blood pressure). In other words, when going from lying down or sitting to standing or walking, the patient will experience the sensation of blood rushing to or from his head (sufficient quantity is actually not being pumped up to his head) due to the fact that his blood pressure drops slightly when he changes position. The body rapidly accommodates this conditon, and the sensation of dizziness or lightheadedness soon passes. He can then go on about his business, since his blood pressure does not usually stay too low. He may feel his heart beat faster or pound just after the head sensation; this is one of the ways the body increases the blood to the head. There is little danger if he is told to change positions *slowly* and to stand for 30 seconds before beginning to walk, after rising from lying or sitting. Unlike the accommodation to sedation, this side effect continues as long as the drug is taken.

*The sugarless part is very important to prevent mouth infections which result from mouth breathing and bacteria which grow in sugar. (Patients mouth-breathe because their noses are stuffed.)

The following side effects are the ones most talked about and overrated in terms of frequency; these are Parkinsonian side effects. "Parkinsonian" refers to the fact that many of the reactions to be described are seen in Parkinson's Disease, which is a complex disorder of certain nerve-cell bodies in the brain. It suffices to say that phenothiazines are thought to cause similar but only temporary disorders in those same brain centers and, hence, cause the side effects seen. (For a fuller understanding see Chapter 14).

*Some* of the Parkinsonian side effects are:

1. a "pill-rolling" motion made with one or both hands, where the thumb is repeatedly and rhythmically moved back and forth across the semiclosed fingers as if the person were dealing cards or rolling pills in his hand. This stops if the hand is used, but will involuntarily begin again if the hand is not being used.

2. a rigid way of walking—rigid gait—where the person looks sort of stiff and may not lift his feet off the floor as before. This is mockingly referred to by chronic, knowledgeable patients as the "Thorazine shuffle." It can be reduced considerably by the addition of anti-Parkinsonian drugs (these will be taken up shortly).

3. akathisia—not true Parkinsonian but commonly seen in side reactions to phenothiazines. This is motor restlessness, an inability to sit still, constant nonrhythmic motion of hands and feet, and subjective complaints such as "can't sit still," "want to move all the time," etc. This is probably the *one most difficult side effect, since it can be misinterpreted* as indicating increasing anxiety, and *more* phenothiazine will be *mistakenly* given. Since anti-Parkinsonian agents do not usually reduce this symptom, the drug dosage must be reduced or a different phenothiazine tried. Obviously, reducing the dosage may cause a recurrence of psychotic symptoms which *can* be differentiated from motor restlessness caused by the drug, but this is a very tricky decision sometimes.

Another almost universally complained of side effect is weight gain. It is really uncertain yet whether phenothiazines merely increase appetite or whether they cause increased accumulation of fat tissue is some metabolic way. In any case, weight gain can become a significant problem with many patients who discover this and then refuse to take the medicine. However, weight gain can be prevented if caloric intake is reduced. Some anti-Parkinsonian agents commonly used are:

| | |
|---|---|
| Artane (trihexiphenidyl) | Kemadrin (procyclidine) |
| Akineton (biperiden) | Cogentin (benztropine) |

These drugs were originally used for Parkinson's disease itself until L-DOPA supplanted them. L-DOPA is not a good drug to use against the side effects of phenothiazines because in various people it induces mood altering effects or other psychological effects which are not beneficial to the person in need of phenothiazines.

Unfortunately, the most disturbing side effects of phenothiazines are not really altered much by the anti-Parkinsonian drugs. That is, blurred vision, weight gain, and akathisia are not usually affected by these agents. However, the tremor of hands, "pill-rolling," rigidity, shuffling gait, etc. can be alleviated with these agents and they are often worth a try. Many M.D.s prescribe these prophylactically with the phenothiazines. This is both unnecessary, since susceptible side effects only occur about 5–10 percent of the time, and unwise, since these agents also *cause* dry mouth, blurred vision, and constipation, and are now thought to contribute to tardive dyskinesia. There are some really rare side effects of which you should be aware in case they occur in one of your patients.

In *either* males or females, breast enlargement and/or lactation may occur (milk or fluid from breasts). Females on high doses of phenothiazines may not menstruate for long intervals. As was mentioned in Chapter 2, men may have no emission of fluid during ejaculation but have no trouble having orgasm (psychosexual pleasure as opposed to physiologic emission). Another occasional side effect of phenothiazines and similar drugs is a severe decrease in, or elimination of, a certain type of white blood cell. These white blood cells are essential to the body in preventing infection; they are called granulocytes and the absence of them in the blood is called agranulocytosis and is potentially fatal. This usually begins as a sore throat and "swollen glands" (under the jaw). There are usually a fever and other symptoms and signs of infection. About 90 percent of the cases of agranulocytosis occur in the first eight weeks of treatment. (Shader and Dimascio, 1970). Therefore, be *especially* alert for complaints of sore throat, "head cold," etc. during this period. Send the patient immediately to a doctor. If sore throat and related symptoms occur at any time during phenothiazine treatment, it is worthwhile getting the patient to a doctor for examination and a "blood count."

## NEUROLOGIC SIDE-EFFECTS

### Acute dystonia

There are two other side effects you may see. Both involve the muscles of the jaw, tongue, and face. These are the acute buccolingual dystonias and tardive dyskinesias. Acute dystonia usually occurs at the beginning of treatment with phenothiazines or the other antipsychotics. It may occur even after one dose. The reaction may also involve the muscles of the neck as well as face. There may be torticollis—a condition in which the neck muscles twist the head around and down with the ear close to the shoulder. Abnormal contraction of the face muscles causes a severely contorted (sometimes one-sided contortion) facial expression. Another type of acute dystonic reaction involving the tongue causes it to swell up and be involuntarily protuded. This is sometimes accompanied by involuntary chewing motions of the jaws. Both acute dystonic reactions can be considerably alleviated by anti-Parkinsonian drugs and antihistamines, both usually given I.M. All three chemical classes of antipsychotic drugs presently on the United States market are capable of producing this reaction.

### Tardive dyskinesia

In 1973 tardive dyskinesia was considered an infrequent complication of prolonged high-dose phenothiazine (and the like) administration, more commonly seen in older women. Even then, it was recognized that tardive dyskinesia could occur after only three to six months of therapy in any age group, any sex, and furthermore, that the risk of tardive dyskinesia is less (A. Jus and Pineau et al.) if the treatment begins at an earlier age. And consequently, regardless of the total dose or duration of treatment, starting phenothiazines at a later age in either sex (women are at greater risk) increases the risk of tardive dyskinesia.

What is tardive dyskinesia? I think a description would help. It is characterized by stereotyped, repetitive, involuntary movements of the mouth, jaw, lips and tongue and is sometimes accompanied by involuntary movements of the limbs or even the trunk. Further, there are sucking and smacking movements of the lips, cheek-puffing, tongue-thrusting and generally abnormal movements of the mouth, jaw and tongue. Also, and very important to distinguish from akathisia, is an inability to sit still—which does not appear alone, but usually with the oral movements described above. The full blown picture is easy to diagnose. It is critical, however, that you learn to 1) be suspicious, 2) *ask* about lip or tongue twitches, 3) watch for ill-defined, abnormal mouth or even eye movements, mild chewing movements, and rocking or swaying, even if apparently voluntary, in order to catch the syndrome before it becomes full blown.

It is estimated that three to six percent of a general psychiatric population would at some time manifest some symptoms of the syndrome. Estimates of over 20 percent prevalence in older psychiatric patients, particularly women, have been made, and I have heard higher prevalence rates than that.

Tardive dyskinesia is a terrible disorder. Some victims never respond to any treatment, although there are many treatments for the disorder. One paradoxical treatment is to *increase* the dose of the phenothiazine (so don't think your consulting M.D. is an idiot). Further, tardive dyskinesia may get worse or *first be seen* after *stopping* the drug. So if your patient has gotten mentally better and the drug has been stopped, particularly in a woman over 45, be especially alert for "tics" and fine abnormal movements of the mouth, lips and tongue. The earlier you catch the tardive dyskinesia, the better the chances for full recovery.

It may occur to you that, if the disorder is so terrible, patients should not be treated with phenothiazines. I think if the patient is dysfunctional in major areas of life, you have to take the risk of tardive dyskinesia. After all, not everybody gets it, and it is often remediable even in older women, *and,* it is hell to live with psychotic symptoms. Obviously, because of the risk, neurotic or other diagnostic categories of people should very rarely be given phenothiazines.

# CHAPTER X

## *Antidepressants*

There are two basic categories of antidepressants, the tricyclic and the monoamine oxidase inhibitors (MAOIs). The theory behind the actions of these drugs is the most developed of any of the biochemical theories we have in psychiatry to explain depression and its possible biochemical causes. (See Chapter 14). It is vital for you to know, however, that recent evidence suggests that different types of depressions respond better either to tricyclics or MAOIs, but that there is also considerable overlap in response by the various depressions.

It is obvious from the outset, therefore, that a careful and thorough diagnosis and history should be made before making any specific suggestion to one's medical back-up. (See Chapter 3 on Depression.) To reiterate very briefly what was said about depression, there are basically three types of depression: major depressive disorder (which may be the first depression or recurrent depression with no history of hypomania), bipolar affective disorder, and neurotic (or "reactive") depression. Major depressive disorder and bipolar may exist with or without psychosis and almost always have consistent sleep and appetite disorders associated with them. Neurotic-reactive depression may be a chronic, life-long characterologic state or a brief episode in reaction to some life experience. In general, neurotic-reactive depressions are not associated with biological signs and MAY NOT RESPOND to either type of antidepressant. Difficulty falling asleep *may* be common in neurotic depression, but it is more closely associated with anxiety and would more likely respond to a minor tranquilizer than to either type of antidepressant. Difficulty falling asleep *in itself* is not considered a major biological sign of depression. This is important, since the majority of outpatients have neurotic/characterologic or reactive depressions. The latter generally subside by themselves in three to six months. A history of depressions during some part of the day or lasting two days with a subsequent return to *normal* mood should infer neurotic depression, not manic-depressive (bipolar) or major depression, both of which generally last until they are treated with drugs (6 months to 20 years), although they sometimes revert by themselves, only to recur later. (There are, however, a few manic-depressives who cycle from severe mania to severe depression within 48 hours.)

In general, major depressive disorder depressions, characterized by sleep loss (particularly early morning awakening, two hours or more early) plus agitation or severe anxiety and/or somatic complaints, combined with loss of appetite and/or weight loss, respond well to *tricyclics*.

The tricyclics are:

Elavil (amitriptyline)
Norpramin (desipramine)
Aventyl (nortriptyline)
Pertofrane (desipramine)
Tofranin (imipramine)
Vivactil (protriptyline)
Sinequan (doxepin)
Surmontil (trimipramine)

The absolutely CARDINAL thing to remember about tricyclic antidepressants and MAOIs is that *response may just BEGIN* in *two* WEEKS or MORE from the date of starting the treatment. It is crucial that the patient who is hoping for an instantaneous cure from his depression be so informed. I generally tell the patient that we will start at a low dose and keep going up at two-week intervals until a definite response or no response is apparent.

Please note that many doctors do not know the correct dosage of these drugs and tend to underdose, thereby giving the ultimate impression that the tricyclic trial has failed. The minimum effective dose for persons under approximately 65 years of age is 100 mg. per day of amitriptyline (Elavil) or imipramine (Tofranil) or the equivalent of the other drugs; exceptions are rare. Combination products which combine small doses of phenothiazines with small doses of tricyclics generally do not contain enough tricyclic to get a good antidepressant response if oversedation with the phenothiazine part is to be avoided. For elderly persons with agitated major depressions, however, these drugs may be quite beneficial since elderly persons often respond to lower doses of tricyclics. At any rate, I usually begin treatment at 100 mg. imipramine or amitriptyline or the equivalent of the other drugs (doxepin 100 mg., desipramine 100 mg., nortriptyline 50 mg., protriptyline 10 mg.) for five days to accustom the patient to the few and mild side effects he may experience. The dose is then raised to 150 mg. of amitriptyline or imipramine or equivalents of the others, and I wait for two weeks. If there is absolutely no improvement in the two weeks, I prescribe 200 mg. and wait another two weeks, and so on up to 300 mg. per day. Again, the dose is not simply dependent on body weight or depth of depression, but is a complex interaction of intestinal absorption, blood level maintenance, blood–brain barrier interactions, and many other factors the majority of which are still unknown. If after the patient reaches 300 mg. for two weeks there is no response, I will wait an additional week or two before considering the drug a failure.

Incidentally, there is now strong evidence for there being a difference between amitriptyline (Elavil) and active metabolites like nortriptyline (Aventyl) and protriptyline (Vivactil), and imipramine and its active metabolites desipramine

(Norpramin, Pertofrane), and trimipramine (Surmontil). It turns out that the imipramine types act more on the norepinephrine neurons, and the amitriptyline types act more on the serotonin neurons. What this means in practice is that if one tricyclic fails, it might be useful to try the other class. There *is* a way to tell which patient will probably respond to which class of tricyclic. It is a urine test which tests for the presence of an end product of norepinephrine metabolism called MHPG. Those coming out high on MHPG will or should respond to Elavil and the like (Serotonegic system). Those coming out low will or should respond to imipramine (Tofranil) and the like. BUT the MHPG test is not widely in use.

So it is a clinical decision which drug to use. The way I make that decision is as follows: If the patient has a retarded, sleep-too-much, eat-too-much, non-agitated depression, I use Tofranil, etc. If the patient has an agitated, loss-of-sleep (particularly early morning awakening) weight-loss depression, I start Elavil, etc. Now, if the patient has sleep-loss but increased appetite, I rely on the sleep factor and start Elavil. This clinical distinction works about 60 to 70 percent of the time. Incidentally, Surmontil allegedly acts on *both* norepinephrine *and* serotonin systems; so I will look for reports in the future.

If both types of tricyclics have failed, it is then MEDICALLY and ETHICALLY IMPERATIVE (in the United States) to wait *at least two weeks more* before MAOIs are attempted after discontinuing the tricyclics. (In England MAOIs and tricyclics are sometiimes used concomitantly. A few deaths are thought to have resulted from the combination, and this has led to the combination being specifically contraindicated.)

This may seem a bit arduous and "trial and error," which it is, but meanwhile the patient is undergoing psychotherapy which, it is to be hoped, sustains him until the drug begins to work. If the diagnosis is correct and the optimum dose is reached, the response, in a few weeks' time, is amazing. Incidentally, in all fairness to everybody's professional ego, such results are more doubtfully obtainable with an equally short term of psychotherapy. (One can never account, however, for placebo reactions," spontaneous remissions, and so-called "transference cures.")

It is also important to keep suicide in mind during the period of deep depression, before the tricyclic begins to work and ESPECIALLY *during the first two weeks after a small response has been noted.* The patient may still be depressed enough to want to kill himself, and now, as he is emerging from the depression, has the "energy" to do it.

A word about bipolar depressions and tricyclics. The bipolar depression, as you may recall, is characterized generally by excessive sleeping (hypersomnia), weight gain, severe energylessness (anergia), with a HISTORY of hypomania or manic episodes at any time in the past. If the depression is so characterized but no hypomanic or manic episodes have yet occurred, the patient must be classified as major depressive disorder, although there is a likelihood that at some time such an episode *will* occur in the future. However, it is generally accepted to start even bipolar depressives on tricyclics first (unless it is known that they previously have *not* responded to up to 300 mg.) due to the greater *potential* toxicity of the MAOIs. If the bipolar depression does not respond within four weeks after initiating therapy, with more rapid rises in dosage to 300 mg. per day, I usually discontinue the tricyclics, *wait two* weeks and initiate treatment with MAO inhibitors. MAO inhibitors are:

Nardil (phenelzine) Marplan (isocarboxazid)
Parnate (tranylcypromine)

What I am about to say is, for the most part, from my own observations, although there have been many reports of the use of MAOIs with borderline, phobic-anxious depersonalized patients, and many of them are contradictory.

Now, one would think that if all the MAO inhibitor does is inhibit MAO (monoamineoxidase enzyme—explained in Chapter 14) then all MAO inhibitors should be the same—but in practice they are not. I think careful diagnosis is the key here and then you can knowledgeably suggest to your consulting M.D. that one or the other be tried.

Clinical example: 40-year-old anorexia nervosa with inability to stop mourning for her husband whom she'd divorced six years ago. She complained of depression, constant crying, inability to cope with her two children and job. Tricyclics (both types) were tried and resulted in such severe anticholinergic side effects that an antidepressant response could not be ascertained because of the dysphoria over the side effects. She had terrible anxiety as well. She was so dysfunctional that she was in danger of losing her job. She gave her kids to her parents and, at home alone, she would "pig out" on junk food and vomit it up. I have always felt that there is a large affective component to anorexia nervosa and she was clearly reactively depressed, without any biological signs. I gave her Nardil, ultimately 60 mg. It was miraculous! She quit the job that was giving her trouble, decided to follow the diet I had given her (to maintain her present weight of 103 pounds) and was able to handle her children again. O.K. She was anxious, depressed reactively for six years and was severely dysfunctional. The anxiety told me not to use Parnate which was excessively stimulative. Nardil was more potent than Marplan and I decided on Nardil. Reactive depression, anxiety, schizoid symptoms all point to Nardil.

Another example: 30-year-old female with clear features of phobias—she couldn't go to a restaurant without feeling claustrophobic and running out, for 10 years; had been to numerous behavior therapists and other psychiatrists for the past 10 years; had anxiety attacks in addition, and had clear symptoms of depersonalization. Now, you might think she is a perfect candidate for psychoanalysis—and indeed she might be, BUT there were no analytic training schools in the area and she could not afford private psychoanalysis. Result: phobic-anxious depersonalization syndrome—treatment, Nardil again, and again miraculous recovery. What happens when you withdraw the drug? That's where meaningful psychotherapy not hampered by excessive anxiety comes in.

I gave slight mention to Parnate as being very stimulating. It differs by *one carbon linkage* from an amphetamine, yet not only is it as stimulating as an amphetamine but it also inhibits

MAO enzymes. As a result it is excellent for nonagitated, excessive sleep-weight gain, and retarded deep depressions. Obviously tricyclics are tried first because of the dietary restrictions with MAO inhibitors, but Parnate is the drug of choice after that. There are also arguments that MAO inhibitors can be ranked from weakest to strongest as follows: Marplan, Nardil, Parnate. This presumably refers to milligram for milligram potency in inhibiting MAO enzyme. However, once the weak MAOI is given in an appropriately high dosage, it should be equal in effect to the more potent MAOIs. However, this in itself needs modification, since MAO enzyme has several forms which may be differentially inhibited by the various MAOIs. In fact there is recent evidence that, because of the differential inhibition, e.g., the brain MAO enzyme vs. the peripheral enzyme, some people can get antidepressant effect yet can eat the MAOI diet-prohibited foods without ill effect. All this is to say that the state of this science is such that we do not know enough to know who will respond to which drug, and that, therefore, although it is unlikely to succeed, it is still worth a try to change from one MAOI to a stronger one, provided that you have waited two weeks in between.

The problem with MAO inhibitors is that the patient must be *extremely reliable.* I mean that he has to follow certain food restrictions or risk the possibility of severe blood pressure increase, which has occasionally caused some deaths or strokes. Bipolar patients may also become hypomanic or manic during treatment with MAOIs, may lose judgment and eat or drink forbidden items. If the patient tends to get too "high" from MAOIs (or tricyclics for that matter), lithium is the treatment of choice, in combination with antidepressants. As you can see, the treatment of manic-depressive illness might initially be better carried out by a psychiatrist or internist familiar with these drugs. Once regulated on lithium with or without antidepressants, psychotherapy can proceed, if warranted, now that the patient's mood swings are regulated. Lithium serum levels after initial regulation should be done at least once a month and should generally be kept at

0.9 mEq/liter to 1.2 mEq/liter; however, some patients respond at both lower and higher serum levels. With lithium (as well as MAOIs) the patient must be extremely reliable since the toxic dose of lithium is exceedingly close to the therapeutic dose and may differ only by one capsule of lithium carbonate. At any rate, except for the dietary restrictions, MAOIs are practically free of side effects and are very valuable for bipolar and some phobic anxious depressions, without psychosis. They may be the only antidepressants that work for certain people and they are invaluable because of this.

The dietary restrictions are as follows:

NO cheese, no liquor of any type, pickled herring, sour cream, yogurt, chicken livers, canned figs, raisins, CHOCOLATE, soy sauce, fava beans or lima beans. Cottage cheese is okay.

There are restrictions *also* on types of medicines NOT to be taken with MAO inhibitors under *any* circumstances. NO cold tablets or cold medicines of *any* type (no nose spray either.) NO amphetamines, diet pills, mood elevators, etc. NO TRICYCLICS (In the United States). NO L-DOPA. NO antihistamines of certain types (The PDR should be referenced.)

Obviously, the patient has to be willing to carry around his list of forbidden foods and drugs. I personally have treated numerous patients as outpatients who were taking MAO inhibitors. I generally tell them that attempting suicide with restricted foods or drugs will generally not result in death (which is true) but may result in severe headache, nosebleeds or stroke, with paralysis possibly leaving them *helplessly* alive. I also give them a great deal of moral support about needing to wait two weeks before the antidepressant effects start, and I see them two or three times a week during this period (as I do with any suicidal patient). Again, the most crucial time is when the patient is just beginning to emerge from the depression. A special problem is the formerly anergic patient who now feels energetic enough to commit suicide and is still depressed enough to want to.

You may begin to think that MAO inhibitors are drastic measures. Certainly, in many respects, tricyclics are potentially safer. But depression, either major or bipolar is a potentially *lethal* disease and somewhat risky measures need to be employed to combat it. With a patient who knows he has your support you can safely give either tricyclics or MAOIs provided the risk of suicide is not so great that the patient ought to be hospitalized. The dose is very variable and depends on which drug is used.

**Side Effects**

The main side effect of both tricyclics and MAOIs is orthostatic hypotension, the same as occurs in phenothiazines. You may remember that orthostatic hypotension is temporarily low blood pressure with change in position from lying down or sitting to standing. Tricyclics also have a high incidence of anticholinergic side effects like dry mouth, stuffy nose, constipation, difficulty in urination, palpitations, etc. They do not generally have "Parkinsonian" side effects although chemically they resemble phenothiazines very closely. Tricyclics have been used, successfully, in combating enuresis (bed wetting) in young boys. They are also used successfully sometimes in severe chronic pain, although the mechanism (aside from the depressing element of chronic pain) is unknown. Tricyclics may cause sedation (amitriptyline (Elavil) and doxepin (Sinequan) are the more sedative, but the others have similiar potential) which may be a rather beneficial side effect in persons with difficulty falling asleep as well as early morning awakening. Tricyclics may also cause blurring of near vision as with phenothiazines. On the other hand, MAOIs, with the exception of diet and drug restrictions and orthostatic hypotension, are virtually free of side effects. They may cause dry mouth or palpitations, but these are less frequent than with tricyclics. One point to note about tranylcypromine (Parnate) in particular is that, possibly because of its resemblance to amphetamine, it can cause difficulty in getting to sleep if taken close to bedtime. I have had patients who complained of difficulty falling asleep with other MAOIs as well. Sometimes taking the total dose before 3 P.M. has been helpful. Since the action of MAOIs does not depend upon maintaining a constant blood level of the drug it can be taken in divided doses, all before 3 P.M. in the afternoon.

## LITHIUM

Lithium is in a class by itself. It is not always an antidepressant by itself, but it clearly protects bipolar patients and some major depressives from recurrence of depression and clearly protects bipolar patients from severe mania. Bipolar patients may cycle or have milder mood swings on lithium.

Lithium is technically not a drug, it is a salt. Do not think that it is a normally occurring trace element which bipolar patients don't have. Lithium is not a trace element in the normal human body. Nobody knows the mechanism of action in the body, but whatever it does, extremely small quantities of lithium are necessary to help depression and mania. Here again, the number of capsules of lithium taken per day has almost no relation to the severity of the illness, so don't make that mistake. It has been found that certain blood levels of lithium are therapeutic, while above and below that level there is either ineffectivenss or toxicity. That level is 0.8 mEQ/liter to 1.2 mEQ/liter. Certain elderly patients do get benefit from 0.5 mEQ/liter but I have never heard of therapeutic effects below that. Above 1.2 mEQ/liter there is danger of nausea, vomiting, diarrhea and worse. ALTHOUGH in acute mania, levels far above that are sometimes necessary. That level is really for maintainance.

Diagnosis is absolutely crucial, and the diagnostic criteria given in earlier chapters should be your guide.

### Side Effects

Lithium is not sedative and has no effect on mental alertness. It has a few side effects, most of which are transient. These are: 1) Diarrhea—comes on in the first week of treatment and may occur at less than therapeutic levels (it lasts about 1 week), nausea or stomach upset after taking the lithium. These are relieved by taking the lithium with meals or with soda or milk and usually disappear in a variable period of time. 2) Tremor of hands—this occurs after about two weeks on lithium and may be quite distressing. *It is not to be taken as a sign of anxiety, but* anxiety makes the tremor worse. The tremor may be transient or persistent. If it is persistent you can suggest to your consulting M.D. that a trial of Inderal 20–60 mg. per day might alleviate the tremor—he may not know that. 3) Edema (swelling of ankles) is an infrequent transient side effect and does not indicate kidney damage from lithium, but it should be evaluated by an M.D. 4) Polydipsia (increased thirst) and polyuria (increased urination) are most common and persistent side effects. They usually persist as long as the salt is taken, but patients accommodate to this rather easily. A salty or metallic taste in the mouth can be a most distressing symptom. Sometimes it is dose-related and sometimes not. It is transient over a period of several months, but during those months the patient will want to get rid of the lithium.

The toxic effects of lithium can *begin* if even only one extra capsule has been taken. They are nausea, vomiting, diarrhea, muscle twiches, staggering and, if severe overdose has been taken, coma and death. Lithium is antithyroid and as such may produce moderate to severe hypothyroidism which may *present to you as depression.* Furthermore, lithium causes weight gain independent of hypothyroidism. Therefore, if a patient who is on lithium starts to complain about weight gain, he needs to have his thyroid checked. If on lithium he also complains of depression, think thyroid. If your patient complains of hair thinning, dry skin or other symptoms (weight gain, slow thinking, deepening voice) he may have hypothyroidism secondary to lithium.

A word about weight gain. This can be substantial and a great cause for concern. In my experience lithium patients need 1000 calories per day or *less* to lose weight. Women in particular may not be able to shed the weight gained on lithium on more than 900 calories per day. That's a pretty stringent diet, and unless they have lithium-induced hypothyroidism, adding some thyroid will not help.

Aside from hypothyroidism and weight gain, and a sometimes long-lasting tremor, lithium has few other side effects of any consequence.

## CANDIDACY FOR LITHIUM

There is a tremendous amount of publicity being given to lithium by some prominent people who have been helped by it. This causes a lot of patients to ask psychotherapists and other mental health professionals whether lithium would be of benefit in their case. Some even come in demanding lithium. Most of the patients who want lithium are depressed, and they think they have heard that lithium works in depression. All the evidence is not in yet, and that which is, is equivocal on whether or not lithium is a good antidepressant, even in bipolar depressions. In general, if a person has had *recurrent* major depressive disorder type of depressions, with or without a history of mania, he should be considered for treatment with lithium. Certainly if he is presently significantly hypomanic or manic with attendant sleep loss, appetite change, weight loss, excess motor activity, etc., he is a prime candidate for lithium. In addition to these more clear-cut indications the situations in which lithium is used or might be used are various and multiple.

Most of the time a person who has had one single episode of depression wants to know if he needs lithium. This really depends upon the psychiatrist who would prescribe the lithium. In a case like this, however, it would indeed be spurious to say that lithium prevented a recurrence of the depression, if we do not know if it would have recurred if *no* treatment were given. I therefore first treat the depression with either tricyclics or MAOIs. Once the depression has responded, I withdraw the antidepressant after a variable period of time. If the depression recurs within three years I use antidepressants again, but would then consider the person for lithium. It is then obvious that there is a relapse without some continuous intervention, which then justifies treatment with a potentially toxic drug like lithium. On the other hand, armed with the knowledge that statistically *50%* of all those suffering major depression will experience recurrences, I wonder if lithium should be the drug of choice on the first episode.

I know that many therapists know of precipitating factors in every recurrent episode of major depression, and that there is a tendency to want to treat this illness with psychotherapy alone. Basically, unfortunately, we try to make symptoms rational, and logically proceed from obvious psychological antecedents. You can find a precipitant for *everything,* if you look hard enough, and if you cannot find one in reality, then the precipitant is unconscious. I do not think the biological extremists or the psychological extremists have enough evidence to come to any major conclusions. *Therefore,* since people who need lithium also need psychotherapy, for the most part, why not use lithium where indicated and also treat them with psychotherapy? At this moment in time, neither we nor the patients can afford to be purists.

# CHAPTER XI

## *Sedatives, Hypnotics, and Narcotic Analgesics*

All the drugs discussed in this chapter are addictive and widely abused by both older and younger generations. It was mentioned that the minor tranquilizers are also addictive in high doses.

Addiction is a complex interaction of *psychological* and *physical dependence* on a drug. Physical dependence denotes an altered state of the physiology of the person such that stoping the drug will result in a characteristic withdrawal or abstinence syndrome. Most withdrawal syndromes have psychological characteristics, but in order for a drug to be considered truly addictive, it must be able to produce physical symptoms of withdrawal, usually having a characteristic pattern for that class of drugs. Other components of addiction as defined by the World Health Organization are: 1) an overwhelming desire or need (compulsion) to continue taking the drug and to *obtain it by any means;* 2) a tendency to increase the dose; 3) a detrimental effect on the individual and on society.

The tendency to increase the dose is due to the phenomenon of tolerance, that is, the original dose of the drug no longer produces the original effect; it produces a decreasing effect, so more and more of the drug has to be taken to obtain the original response. In general, if a person is tolerant to one specific drug, say Seconal (a barbiturate), he will be tolerant to all barbiturates, and may also be tolerant to other drugs which produce the *same* effects even though they are chemically different. Another point of interest is that drugs that produce the *same effects* (even though chemically dissimilar) will produce very similar withdrawal symptoms.

One very good point to remember is that *withdrawal syndromes produce symptoms which are the direct opposite of the usual effects of the drug.* For example, barbiturates generally depress nervous excitability, so you can expect that the withdrawal from barbiturates will cause increased excitability, nervousness and irritability. This will be clearer when each class of drugs has been discussed.

## SEDATIVES AND HYPNOTICS, TYPE I: BARBITURATES

A sedative is a drug that is supposed to decrease excitement and anxiety without producing marked drowsiness. Hypnotic, for our purposes, is really a misnomer and actually should be called soporific or simply sleep-producing. Barbiturates are medically used as both sedatives and sleeping-pills. Whether they act as a sedative or produce sleep depends on the dose. Unfortunately, even in small doses most patients complain of drowsiness when a barbiturate is prescribed to calm anxiety.

Barbiturates are much abused in today's society. They are used to get intoxicated ("high") and they are used to sleep by many, as part of what I call the "up and down" syndrome—amphetamines during the day ("ups" as they are called) and barbiturates at night ("downs") because the person cannot sleep at night due to the "ups" he took during the day and cannot wake up in the morning due to the "downs" he took the night before.

Here is a lilst of the trade and "street" names of the most commonly prescribed and, for that matter, abused, barbiturates. Their most common medical use is also listed. Many other preparations, not used exclusively as sedatives or sleeping-pills, contain barbiturates, but that list is too long to be included. Barbiturates in general are called downs, goofballs, barbs, and idiot pills.

| *Brand Name* | *Medical Use* | *Street Names* |
|---|---|---|
| Butisol (butabarbital) | sedative and sleep | |
| Luminal (phenobarbital) | sedative and sleep | |
| Amytal (amobarbital) | sedative and sleep | |
| Seconal (secobarbital) | sleep | red devils, red birds red 88's, reds |
| Nembutal (pentobarbital) | sleep | yellow jackets, nemmies |
| Tuinal (secobarbital plus amobarbital) | sleep | double trouble, rainbows, tooies |

## The Effects of Barbiturates

At the most basic level, barbiturates interfere with certain groups of cells in the brain which are responsible for alertness. A barbiturate is one kind of central nervous system depressant; that is, it tends to depress (slow down, decrease) many functions of the brain and spinal cord (which, taken together, are called the central nervous system). As far as we are concerned here, barbiturates slow down speech, respiration, body movements, thinking, and the capacity to verbalize thoughts. People intoxicated ("stoned") on barbiturates look very much the same as though they were drunk on alcohol. Balance is impaired, they may stagger or drag their feet, their eyes look sort of half-open or drowsy, and their movements may be uncoordinated. However, many addicts can take barbiturates all day long, and although they are psychologically "high," they somehow manage not to show most of the signs of intoxication, except if you are very alert to a slight slurring of speech and a slight slowing of their ability to verbalize thoughts.

An overdose of barbiturates can produce anything from prolonged sleep to death by respiratory arrest (the center in the brain controlling automatic breathing simply stops; the person already sleeping or in a coma stops breathing). A good rule of thumb for patients who need sleeping pills and are suicidal is that one week's supply (usually seven pills) is unlikely to cause death even if taken all at once. However, the effects of alcohol, tranquilizers, narcotics, and nonbarbiturate sleeping-pills are additive to the effect of barbiturates. Therefore, keep these additive effects in mind when assessing the suicidal potential of a given prescription.

The person addicted to barbiturates of any type is tolerant to them and tends to take as many as he can get his hands on. He will also consume nonbarbiturate sleeping pills since they have the same effect and, hence, he is tolerant to them also (crosstolerance).

The clinical description of barbiturate intoxication has already been presented. It should be noted that it is very similar to alcohol intoxication, and that, like alcoholics, barbiturate addicts can hide most of the clinical effects from you.

## A Further Note On Effects

Unlike the effects of chronic alcohol intoxication, which can be permanent brain and liver damage, and a host of other permanent damages, chronic barbiturate intoxication *of itself* is not to my knowledge associated with any *permanent* damage to any organ or to the brain. No matter how long the patient has been addicted or chronically intoxicated, once he is safely withdrawn, there do not seem to be permanent ill effects. The problem is that, as with heroin and alcohol addiction, the life style and eating habits of the barbiturate addict deteriorate. There is general body neglect and often disease if the addict injects the drugs by vein. Also, many addicts suffer from vitamin deficiencies and very poor dental hygiene.

Permanent brain damage can result, however, from overdosage, with ensuing coma and an inadequate supply of oxygen caused by too shallow breathing for too long. Brain damage can also result from uncontrolled convulsions which can result from barbiturate withdrawal.

If your patient admits to barbiturate addiction, or if you suspect he is addicted, you must remember one absolutely unbreakable rule: NEVER, UNDER ANY CIRCUMSTANCES, TELL A BARBITURATE ADDICT OR SOMEONE WHO TAKES LARGE DOSES OF MINOR TRANQUILIZERS TO STOP TAKING BARBITURATES (OR MINOR TRANQUILIZERS) ABRUPTLY. ABRUPT WITHDRAWAL OF BARBITURATES CAN RESULT IN UNCONTROLLABLE CONVULSIONS AND DEATH. A barbiturate addict cannot go "cold turkey." If he wants to withdraw, he should be kept in a hospital where access to supply is limited and where he can be gradually withdrawn safely.

You may come across a patient addict who does not know the above fact, and he may decide to stop taking his bartiburates abruptly. If the withdrawal syndrome has already begun, he will be irritable, hypersensitive to environmental stimuli (e.g., noise), highly anxious, tremulous, and may complain of nausea and abdominal pain. If he is further into withdrawal he may present signs of delirium, i.e., confusion, memory impairment, disorientation, as well as hyperirritability. In any case, as a stop-gap measure, tell him to take one or two barbiturates immediately, and then get him to a hospital right away because all of these signs precede convulsions.

## A Rough Guide to Tell If Your Patient Is Addicted

A person can be mildly physically dependent on as few as two Nembutal, Seconal or Tuinal per day, in that he might experience hyperexcitability and nervousness if he suddenly stops taking them. If he is only taking two per day every day, he is *unlikely* to experience convulsions upon withdrawal. If a patient is taking only one or two barbiturates a day and *does not* tend to increase the dose, but wants to continue them for sleep and does *not* get withdrawal symptoms if he doesn't take them, he is said to be habituated. Habituation involves *psychological* but not *physical dependence.*

In my own practice I would even hesitate to tell a patient who I felt I was absolutely *sure* was taking *only* two barbiturates a day to stop taking them, because the likelihood is that if a patient is admitting to two a day, he is probably taking four or more a day, so it is advisable to get him into a drug detoxification unit at a hospital if he wants to withdraw.

There is no upper limit to the number of pills per day that defines addiction, but four Seconal, Nembutal or Tuinal per day can produce a clinically significant physical dependence.

In true addiction, the tendency is to increase the dose of one specific drug, or take other drugs whose effects are the same in combination—whatever the addict can get his hands on. In trying to assess a patient's drug intake be sure to ask about nonbarbiturate sleeping pills and minor tranquilizers, etc.

There are no real *clinical* signs of barbiturate *addiction* per se, if the drugs are not injected, but there are those signs of intoxication and withdrawal which we have mentioned. If a patient suddenly complains of anxiety, irritability and hypersensitivity to noise, light, etc. ask him if he had been taking barbiturates and stopped, even if he never admitted it to you before. You may save his life.

## SEDATIVES AND HYPNOTICS, TYPE II NONBARBITURATE PRESCRIPTION DRUGS

The most commonly prescribed drugs in this category of nonbarbiturate sleeping preparations are:

| | |
|---|---|
| Chloral hydrate | (This is the generic name) |
| Paraldehyde | (This is the generic name) |
| Placidyl | (ethchlorvynol) |
| Valmid | (ethinamate) |
| Doriden | (glutethimide) |
| Noludar | (methyprylon) |
| Dalmane | (flurazepam) |
| Quaalude | (methaqualone) |

The drugs covered in this section are generally medically used for sleep rather than as antianxiety sedatives. They all have additive effects with alcohol, tranquilizers, barbiturates, and narcotics. Some are chemically very similar to barbiturates, others are very different, but all have the capacity to induce sleep or intoxication in chronic abusers and all are addictive. In general, addicts who are tolerant to barbiturates will be tolerant to these drugs too, and vice versa. Most do not, in themselves, produce any permanent organ or brain damage, even after years of chronic ingestion or intoxication. The withdrawal symptoms in general are very similar to those produced by discontinuance of barbiturates and the same warning is given here as is given for those drugs: NEVER TELL A SLEEPING-PILL ADDICT TO ABRUPTLY STOP TAKING SLEEPING-PILLS AS THIS CAN RESULT IN UNCONTROLLABLE CONVULSIONS AND DEATH.

In general, the results of overdosage with nonbarbiturate sleeping-pills are the same as those with barbiturates, namely, anything from prolonged sleep to coma and death by respiratory arrest.

You may have been wondering why there are different types of barbiturates and why, if the effects are so similar, the nonbarbiturate sleeping pills were developed at all. Free enterprise is one answer, but also the drugs do vary in their speed of onset of action, how long they keep the person asleep, and how fast they are eliminated by the body. Some of these variables determine, for example, how much of a "hangover" a given drug produces the following day. Also, there is always the problem of allergy to barbiturates and individual drug sensitivities, tolerances, or preferences.

## NARCOTIC-ANALGESICS: OPIUM DERIVATIVES AND SYNTHETIC NARCOTICS

Opium is derived from the unripe seed capsules of the opium poppy (Papaver somniferum). Two of the natural products of opium have narcotic (producing numbness and/or lethargy) and analgesic (pain relieving) effects. These are morphine and codeine. Heroin is produced synthetically from morphine and is also a very potent narcotic-analgesic. In fact, heroin was once introduced as a cure for addiction to morphine, having all of its pain-relieving qualities, but allegedly none of its addicting properties. Unfortunately, this was not so, and science is still searching for the potent analgesic that is nonaddicting. All of the drugs in the following list are addictive. Many are synthetically derived from morphine or codeine and others are entirely synthetically produced. All of the drugs are cross tolerant with each other—every single one of them. An addict can take any one of them for at least partial relief from withdrawal symptoms due to another. The list is long and may contain a surprise or two, like Darvon (Darvon is weakly addictive), but it will serve as a reference in case one of your patients has had one of them prescribed, became mildly addicted, and begins to experience withdrawal symptoms.

| | |
|---|---|
| Dilaudid | (hydromorphone) |
| Percodan | (oxycodone is the narcotic, but Percodan also contains aspirin, phenacetin and caffeine |
| Demerol | (meperidine) |
| Dolophine | (methadone) (Prescription limited in U.S.) |
| Darvon | (Propoxyphene) |
| Codeine | generic |
| Morphine | generic |
| Heroin | (cannot be prescribed (generic) in U.S.) |

There are many others, but these are the most common.

### The Effects of Narcotic-Analgesics

All of the drugs on the above list are powerful pain relievers, but some are much less potent than others in the usualy prescribed dose. Depending upon the circumstances they relieve anxiety and fear as well. Morphine and heroin, and to a lesser extent all the others, are said by addicts to produce euphoria, but many persons respond negatively to the feeling-state produced by these drugs. They also very frequently cause drowsiness, dizziness, and nausea. All produce constipation and to some extent may cause difficulty in urinating and/or a decrease in urine volume. All are powerful respiratory depressants, and death from overdosage is almost always due to respiratory arrest. Morphine and heroin, and to a lesser extent the rest of the drugs, markedly decrease sexual desire and may also delay ejaculation or inhibit it completely. An important clinical note is that heroin and morphine, as well as some of the others, produce very marked constriction of the pupils; a telltale sign of whether a patient has had a dose within the last four hours. One exception is Demerol which produces dilitation (widening) of the pupils.

It is again interesting that chronic abuse of these drugs does *not* cause permanent damage to any organ or the brain in and of itself. However, because many addicts inject the drugs into their veins, hepatitis (liver infection) and infection of the lining of the heart (bacterial endocarditis) often occur due to the lack of sterile conditions during injection, and can result in permanent damage to these organs. Continuous injection in the same vein—even with a sterile needle—can result in inflammation and clotting of the blood in the vein.

There are no definite, always present, outward signs of addiction per se, but certain points are worth mentioning. Needle tracks on the arms or legs may present. These are often long, reddened or darker-colored streaks which follow the course of veins, on the skin of the forearm or inside portion of the ankles and calves. Many addicts *always* wear long sleeved shirts, even in summer, to hide these tracks, plus wearing sunglasses indoors to hide constriction of the pupils. These signs should alert you, but many addicts inject under the skin ("skin-popping") and do not have needle tracks. However, "skin-poppers" often have many boils and small infections on their arms. An addict who has just injected heroin may have slurred speech, incoordination and slow thinking or verbalization, just as a barbiturate addict or alcoholic may have. But I have seen hundreds of addicts who, except for needle tracks or constricted pupils, show no other outward signs of having just injected.

## The Abstinence (Withdrawal) Syndrome Characteristic for Drugs Listed

Heroin will be used as a model, but these symptoms occur upon withdrawal of any of the drugs listed, if the patient is addicted.

The symptoms usually begin 6–12 hours after the last dose. They are: yawning, eyes tearing, nose dripping clear fluid, and sweating. Later on, over the next 12–24 hours, the patient gets muscle cramps and muscle twitches, hot and cold flashes, chills and dilitation of the pupils.* (Since many of the early signs are subjective and can be faked, I never believe an addict who complains he is in withdrawal unless his pupils are dilated.) About 36–48 hours after the last dose, the patient will vomit, wretch, have diarrhea, refuse to eat or drink very much, and will continue to twitch and complain of pain in his back and legs. On about the third day after the last dose most of these symptoms will have subsided, but the patient may continue to complain of weakness, back and leg pain or cramps, insomnia and restlessness for days to weeks after withdrawal.

As you can see, this withdrawal syndrome is not nearly as dangerous as the convulsions that ensue from sleeping-pill withdrawal, and many addicts have gone through it without medical aid ("cold turkey"). It *is* more humane, however, to have the patient admitted to a drug detoxification center than to let him go "cold turkey."

## Methadone

Methadone and methadone maintenance are the subjects of considerable controversy. Methadone is pharmacologically similar to morphine and heroin in that it is addictive and it alleviates pain. It is much longer-acting than morphine and is said not to produce the same "high" as heroin. Methadone has also been said to be capable of "blocking" the "high" from heroin if taken before it. Methadone is crosstolerant with all the drugs listed and can be used as a substitute for them to lessen withdrawal symptoms. The one advantage of methadone is that it can be taken orally but, aside from heroin, so can all the other drugs listed. It is interesting to think about why society and the medical community sanction methadone for maintenance as opposed to any other of the

*Demerol is the exception. Constriction occurs when this drug is used.

oral drugs, or why, if it is so similar to heroin and as addictive, we do not have heroin maintenance. There are really many arguments pro and con about methadone and heroin maintenance, but these are quite beyond the scope of this book.

Maintenance means just what it says: The addict is placed on high doses of methadone initially to substitute for his heroin habit and gradually the dosage is decreased but not discontinued, and the addict then comes to a methadone maintenance center for his daily dose. Many addicts feel that methadone prevents their craving for heroin, and since it is legal and free, they do not have to engage in illegal activities to obtain either the heroin or money to get it.

# CHAPTER XII

## *Psychotomimetics*

The drugs discussed in this chapter are all capable of producing hallucinations, one of the hallmarks of psychosis. However, they can produce profound alterations in thinking and mood as well, which can be indistinguishable from psychotic states—hence, they are called psychotomimetic rather than merely hallucinogenic.

Psychotomimetic drugs produce sensory illusions (distortions of perception based on some object or occurrence in reality), hallucinations (sensory perceptions generated entirely by the mind), distortions of time sense and body image, increased vividness of perception, memory or fantasy, and depersonalization (the subject feels strangely detached from himself and may feel that he is watching himself going through the experience). Changes in mood generally go in the direction of euphoria, but on "bad trips" there can be profound depression or panic. Delusions occur also and can be mild (flashes of great "insight" which later turn out to be gibberish) or severe (wherein the person feels people are out to kill him or that he is going to die, etc.). Protracted psychotic reactions do occur with these drugs and these are, or are sometimes indistinguishable from, acute schizophrenic states. There is some evidence that schizophrenic reactions following these drugs are not really caused by them, but merely released by the drugs. (A protracted reaction is usually considered to be one where the person is still either hallucinating, delusional, panicked or depressed, etc., three days after drug ingestion.)

With the exception of amphetamines, none of the psychotomimetics cause physical dependence, nor do they have abstinence syndrome. Prolonged and high-dose use of these drugs can lead to personality changes which are slowly becoming recognized as "loss of motivation" syndromes.

## LSD, MESCALINE, DMT, STP (DOM), PSILOCYBIN, NUTMEG, DOET, PCP

These drugs are grouped together because they are essentially similar in effects. (STP and DOET are really amphetamine derivatives, but are more closely allied to the others than to prescribable amphetamines as they will be discussed later in this chapter.) It is important to realize that psychosis *is* the *usual* (and usually desired) effect of these drugs, produced by *one* sufficient dose of the drug. This is in contrast to amphetamines and marijuana which *are* psychotomimetic, but psychosis is *not* the *usual* or expected response with one dose.

The drugs are generally taken orally and rarely (except STP) if ever injected. They take effect usually within one hour if an ample dose is taken. At first there are some sympathetic effects—pupil dilitation, increased heart rate, and increased blood pressure. Soon the psychotomimetic effects begin and the subject usually feels euphoric and may begin to have visual illusions like walls undulating or his feet going further away from him. He may then begin to hallucinate. It is interesting that with psychotomimetics, unlike psychosis itself, the subject usually retains the insight that the experiences he is undergoing are unreal. Occasionally the person on LSD, STP or the other drugs may show signs of acute organic brain syndrome with its disorientation and memory impairment. In that case the state would be called a toxic psychosis. Usually, however, the subject knows where he is and what day it is, but is too distracted by his hallucinations or his euphoria to tell you.

Flashbacks can occur with any of these drugs. These are the occurrence of illusions, delusions, hallucinations or any other components of the psychedelic experience days, weeks or months *after* the *last ingestion.* I had a patient who had taken amphetamines and LSD rather steadily for a month, and was still complaining of walls undulating, wallpaper patterns "flowing" and depersonalization two years after his last ingestion. In this case, as in many others, it is likely that his psychopathology was released by the drug rather than caused by it.

There is no treatment necessary for the ingestion of these drugs, unless the person is panicked or is on a "bad trip" and wants relief. Overdose is rare, but can warrant medical attention mostly for the psychological ill effects. If you have a patient who is having a "bad trip," the best thing to do is get him to the emergency room of a hospital. There he will be treated with phenothiazines or benzodiazepines to which most of the drug-effects respond. The treatment of a patient who has had a schizophrenic reaction following LSD or other drug ingestion is generally the same as if it were not apparently initiated by the drug experience. The patient is treated with phenothiazines and the appropriate psychotherapy.

## Long-Range Effects

Certainly, all the evidence is not in yet, and the evidence which *is* in is contradictory. Some studies have shown increases in chromosomal breakage in LSD users. Other studies found no difference in frequency of such breakage between users and nonusers. Memory defects have been found by some investigators, and are disputed by others. I have personally had patients who *complain* of memory defects years after heavy LSD use, but these defects are very difficult to demonstrate on objective testing.

While subtle changes in memory and other intellectual functions may be difficult to document, psychological changes have been well documented. At the present time there is no doubt that the most serious *known* possible consequence of psychotomimetic drug use (whether one dose or heavy use) is protracted psychotic disturbance, markedly resembling schizophrenia. It is difficult to know in such cases whether the "schizophrenia" is a drug effect, or a latent process which has been uncovered or released by the drug. Some studies show that protracted reactions occur usually after high doses or prolonged usage in persons who have a history of previous psychological or neurological disturbance. However, even this is disputed, and other studies indicate that prolonged psychotic reactions occur in persons with no previous psychiatric history.

Most of the studies have been done on LSD users. This does not detract from the psychotogenic potential of the other drugs, and in a way, may even enhance it. This is because few LSD users use only LSD, and often combine it with mescaline, amphetamines or STP. It therefore becomes difficult to know which drug has caused the protracted psychosis. It is safe to say that *any* psychotomimetic is capable of producing or uncovering a schizophrenic-like syndrome which may last for weeks to months or even years after ingestion.

Amphetamines are very widely used and abused by all segments of the population, from college students to doctors and nurses to dieters everywhere. All the drugs on the following list are legal by prescription in the United States, but are presently *controlled drugs,* much like morphine and barbiturates. The *more* psychotogenic amphetamine derivatives (STP, DOET) are not legally prescribable. However, amphetamines and cogeners of the type discussed in this section *are definitely psychotomimetic.* The difference is that the prescribable amphetamines and cogeners do *not regularly* and usually produce hallucinations, illusions, etc. with *one* dose. In order to obtain psychotic reactions from these, high and frequent doses must be taken. These amphetamines, however, are *addicting*. They produce a withdrawal syndrome whose symptoms are indicative of psychological and physical dependence. As with any addictive drug, tolerance develops, so the user must increase his dose in order to get the same effect.

## AMPHETAMINES AND AMPHETAMINE-COGENERS

| *Trade Names* | | | |
|---|---|---|---|
| *Amphetamines* | *Generic* | *"Street" Name* | *General Names* |
| Benzedrine<br>Dexedrine<br>Bontril | (amphetamine sulfate) | bennies | "ups," pep pills |
| Amodex | (dextroamphetamine) | dexies | speed, diet pills, white crosses |
| Obotan<br>Bamadex | | | |
| Desbutal<br>Desoxyn<br>Fetamin<br>Obedrine | (methamphetamine) | meth, crystal | |
| Biphetamine | (amphetamine and dextroamphetamine) | black beauties | cross countries |
| *Amphetamine Cogeners* | | | |
| Ritalin | (methyphenidate) | | |
| Preludin | (phenmetrazine) | | |

Amphetamines are central nervous system stimulants, and their effects physiologically closely parallel sympathetic stimulation. That is, they cause nervousness, irritability, loss of appetite, insomnia, increased blood pressure, increased heart rate, sweating, and pupil dilitation. It is from some of these properties that the amphetamines derive their medical uses. They are often prescribed for weight reduction because of their ability to suppress appetite. The appetite-supression effect is very short-lived, however, so that amphetamines can only be taken effectively for dieting for about two weeks. Amphetamines are also prescribed to help keep people awake who suffer from a type of epilepsy in which the patient gets attacks of sleep (narcolepsy). Most unfortunately, amphetamines or cogeners are frequently prescribed for temporary relief of depression. Here again, their effect lasts only about two weeks. If no more long-lasting antidepressant is prescribed during the course of the amphetamines, the person may feel as bad or worse at the end of those two weeks due to the letdown secondary to the reduced effectiveness of the amphetamines as when he began.

Aside from their questionable use in dieting, there is another legitimate and beneficial use for amphetamines in psychiatry—to lift the spirits of patients on tricyclics during the period of two weeks or so until the tricyclic takes effect. Since their effect lasts only about four to six hours, a twice-a-day 5 mg. tablet must be taken. As previously indicated they *must not* be taken with MAO inhibitors.

Psychologically, amphetamines produce euphoria, increased sexual drive, excitement, "high," or fearfulness, ideas of reference, paranoid feelings, hallucinations, delusions, and violent impulsive behavior, depending upon the dose, frequency of the dose and whether the use is one dose or chronic. In an experiment, "normal" volunteers were given amphetamines intravenously (by vein) until psychosis was reached. All the subjects experienced a paranoid psychosis almost indistinguishable from paranoid schizophrenia within two to five days of continuous hourly infusion. Before becoming psychotic, however, all the subjects went through a period of depression and social withdrawal, even though they were still receiving the amphetamine.

Chronic abuse of amphetamines in high doses can interfere with mental functioning and motivation for several years after withdrawal. As with any addiction, deterioration in health and social functioning occurs, and this is worsened by the poor appetite and insomnia caused by the drug. The danger of inducing a paranoid schizophrenic-like syndrome remains ever present if amphetamines are used in high doses over time.

It is very interesting that the above statements apply only to *adults*. Amphetamines or cogeners are prescribed in frequent doses to very young children who are "hyperactive" presumably as a result of minimal brain damage. In children as well as adults, amphetamines act to increase attention span and ability to concentrate. This combination tends to make the child appear less hyperactive and distractable. Children treated with relatively high doses (for them) do not usually become psychotic even with treatment over long periods of time.

### Amphetamine Withdrawal

Although the full physiological and psychological withdrawal syndrome occurs only after tolerance and addiction have developed, even one dose or occasional use of amphetamines can result in a post-drug depression or lethargy. This is why these drugs should not be used as long term antidepressants. The full withdrawal syndrome is a psychological disaster. As if it were not enough that high frequent doses produce a paranoid psychosis during abuse, withdrawal also produces a paranoid psychosis, equally indistinguishable from paranoid schizophrenia. Frightening hallucinations, both auditory and visual, occur and paranoid delusions are common. Extreme lethargy, depression, and fatigue are the rule, since these are the direct opposite effects of the drug. The amphetamine addict who is "crashing" may sleep for several days, but this sleep is disturbed both physiologically and psychologically. Terrifying nightmares occur, and EEG recordings demonstrate severe abnormalities of REM sleep (rapid eye movement stage of sleep) during this period. Headaches, profuse sweating, and severe muscle cramping accompany the psychological symptoms. Even if psychotic symptoms do not occur, withdrawal is marked by severe depression, and terrifying thoughts or feelings.

The amphetamine abstinenence psychosis generally begins a few days after discontinuing use, but this reaction has been known to occur as long as two months later. It usually lasts about a week, but again, it may persist for months or years and progress to a chronic phase indistinguishable from paranoid schizophrenia.

Obviously, an amphetamine addict who wants to withdraw should be withdrawn in a hospital, not only because psychosis may possibly occur, but because the depression which accompanies the withdrawal presents a significant suicide risk.

## COCAINE

Cocaine is a central nervous system stimulant and resembles action of amphetamines very closely. It does not, however, produce physical dependence or tolerance. It does produce one of the strongest cravings known in drug abuse. Craving may be an as yet unmeasurable physiological response, but it is certainly a marked psychological response. Cocaine, amphetamines, and heroin are about equal in their ability to produce almost overwhelming desire for themselves long after cessation. This craving is so strong that it usually leads to resumption of abuse, even though cocaine is not physically addicting.

Cocaine produces the familiar sympathetic effects noted for amphetamines, but in addition has the capacity to produce convulsions. It *is* psychotomimetic and large doses can produce delusions, hallucinations, and paranoid ideation.

## MARIJUANA AND HASHISH

Marijuana and hashish come from plants of the genus *cannabis*. The active ingredient in both plants is tetrahydrocannabinol or THC. It is THC which produces the psychoactive effects of these two drugs. Hashish has the higher content of THC. THC is found in different quantities in different parts of the plant. In general the THC content is found in decreasing quantity in the following parts: resin, flowers, leaves. There is practically no THC in the stems, roots or seeds. Jamaican ganja is more potent than marijuana because it is made from the flower tops and some leaves. Hashish is made exclusively from the resin and is the most potent of the THC-containing drugs.

Since the psychoactive ingredient is THC, both drugs exert similar effects on the mental functioning of the user. Hashish will produce a greater effect and last longer since it contains more THC than the other products.

The route by which the drugs are taken generally affects the time lapse until drug effect is felt and the duration of the response, but all routes—generally smoking or eating—will ultimately produce a response if sufficient quantity is taken. High doses can be psychotomimetic.

Psychotic phenomena such as hallucinations, mild delusions, distortion of body image, and loss of sense of identity can occur. Also, and not to be confused with psychotic phenomena, panic reactions or anxiety reactions can occur, especially in novice users. These reactions occur when the person is afraid that his sense of subjective self-control is lost, or is terrified that he is losing his mind or sense of identity. Both psychotic phenomena and panic reactions clear rapidly as the THC is eliminated from the body.

Tolerance to THC (by long-term users) is said (by them) to occur, but apparently physical addiction does not. There are claims for both straight tolerance, i.e., more drug needed to produce usual response, and "reverse tolerance," i.e., *less* drug needed the more was consumed on previous occasions. In recent months I have heard arguments for both possibilities. The arguments are usually based on how rapidly different metabolites are excreted or stored. Psychological dependence does occur where the taking of the drug becomes a compulsive necessity in order to "feel good" or even "feel normal." This leads to drug-seeking behavior which is tantamount to the type of drug-seeking behavior found with drugs, like heroin, which are physically addicting.

The Marijuana Commission Report National Commission (1972) does not conclusively state that brain injury occurs with extremely heavy use. They do note, however, that pulmonary (lung) function is decreased as with any chronic smoking, but mostly in those who smoke regular cigarettes.

Studies done in other countries where hashish has been smoked heavily for periods of 20 years or more indicate evidence of motivation changes and other changes in behavior which accommodate the drug-seeking and compulsive behaviors associated with very heavy use.

With *intermittent "social"* use, *no behavioral, physical,* or *mental changes* could be demonstrated. This is also true of alcohol, the deleterious effects of chronic use of which are more clear-cut than those for long-term heavy ingestion of THC. It is interesting that the Commission on Marijuana recommended continued prohibition of marijuana essentially because of the risk of increasing the number of long-term heavy users; despite the fact that the predominant use in this country is short-term and intermittent. The Commission concluded that the existing social and legal policies relating to marijuana use were out of proportion to the demonstrable social or physical harm which could come from such use. This is in marked contrast to society's view of alcohol, the deleterious effects of which on mind and body are all very well known, but whose use is unrestricted.

# CHAPTER XIII

# *Alcohol and Alcoholism*

Alcohol is a central nervous system depressant. As you may recall from other chapters, this means that it slows down the functions of higher and lower brain and spinal cord centers. It is similar, therefore, to major and minor tranquilizers, barbiturates, narcotics, and nonbarbiturate sleeping pills. It is additive to the effects of any of these other drugs. It is psychologically and physically addictive in that there is a specific withdrawal syndrome that occurs if the addicted person stops drinking suddenly. Overdoses *usually* produce sleep before the person can drink enough to suppress his respiration enough to cause death, but overdose can produce death by respiratory arrest. Also, death by respiratory arrest can and often does occur when alcohol is combined with other CNS depressants either by accident or design. In small doses, alcohol is a minor tranquilizer in that it produces emotional relaxation for a short period of time. It is also a vasodilator, that is, it causes the capillaries in the skin to open up wider and thereby produces the feeling of warmth associated with small dose consumption. Actually the capillaries are letting out heat by dilating, thus really cooling the body. Alcohol, like other CNS depressants, lowers body temperature by suppressing the higher regulatory center for body temperature, as well as by vasodilatation.

In the withdrawal syndrome, this pattern is reversed, and fever is associated with other symptoms of withdrawal. These symptoms are: coarse tremors, hallucinations, convulsions, and an acute organic brain syndrome. The entire withdrawal syndrome is called rightly *delirium tremens* or the *D.T.s.* This is so aptly called *delirium tremens* because the most prominent symptoms are delirium, i.e., an acute organic brain syndrome with disorientation, memory impairment, impaired judgment, and intellectual deficits, *and* tremors, very gross shaking of the limbs such that the patient literally can not hold a glass of water and drink from it, plus visual hallucinations. It only occurs where a person is addicted to alcohol, and not merely from an overdose on one occasion.

D.T.s is associated with about a 20% mortality rate despite good treatment. *It is as dangerous to tell an alcoholic on a binge to stop drinking suddenly as it is to tell a barbiturate addict to stop taking barbiturates suddenly.* In fact, the withdrawal syndromes resemble each other, particularly in the danger of precipitating convulsions if withdrawal is abrupt. It is not even necessary that the alocholic stop drinking suddenly in order to produce D.T.s. It is known to occur when the alcoholic has merely reduced his intake while continuing to drink. If the alcoholic wants to stop or "dry out" it is best done in a hospital where anticonvulsant medication can be given prophylactically.

## ALCOHOL ADDICTION: ALCOHOLISM

How can you tell if a person is addicted to alcohol? If you question him about how he uses alcohol; whether or not he has experienced the "shakes" in the morning or hallucinations (if he does not have hallucinations *off* alcohol) while drinking or after stopping drinking, etc. The National Committee on Alcoholism defines major and minor criteria for the diagnosis of alcoholism. The major criteria are associated with the evidence of physical addiction as manifested by the production of withdrawal symptoms (shakes, hallucinations or full blown D.T.s), and the manifestations of alcohol-related disease in the blood, liver, and other organ systems of the body. The major psychological criteria defining psychological dependence are: 1) drinking despite strong medical advice to the contrary; 2) drinking despite known social consequences such as loss of job, loss of spouse, loss of driver's license, etc.); 3) patient's subjective evaluation that he has lost control of his alcohol consumption.

In addition to the major psychological and physical criteria, there are minor criteria which are *often* associated with alcoholism, but greatly depend on the peer group habits of the patient. The National Committee on Alcoholism (as printed in the *American Journal of Psychiatry,* August 1972) lists the following signs, about which the patient should be questioned, as suggestive of the diagnosis of alcoholism: gulping drinks, drinking in the morning, surreptitious drinking, repeated attempts at abstinence, repeated and multiple medical excuses from work, preference for companions who drink or for bars and taverns, loss of interest in activities not directly associated with drinking, frequent car accidents, frequent changes in residence for poorly defined reasons, outbursts of rage or suicidal gestures while drinking, drinking to relieve anger, insomnia, fatigue, depression or social discomfort and psychological symptoms consistent with permanent organic brain syndrome (see Korsakoff's Psychosis). There are many other *late* criteria but these are the early and middle stage signs of alcoholism.

In general, if you have a rapport with the patient, he may feel comfortable enough to admit his subjective fears that he has lost control of his alcohol consumption. It is very difficult to correctly diagnose if the patient blatantly denies any of the above signs despite his knowledge to the contrary. Often, none of those signs are acknowledged as present if the patient is a binge drinker or "weekend-alcoholic," i.e., he only gets drunk on weekends or only has the signs during binges which he may or may not admit.

There is another type of drinker, one who is said to have pathological intoxication, for he gets violently drunk or behaviorally very different after one or two normal size drinks. This type of person may or may not be an alcoholic. Usually the behavior following one or two drinks is extremely different from the person's normal behavior. He may be violent or verbally abusive, he may cry or be suicidal or extremely impulsive. He may also suffer a "blackout"; this also occurs to alcoholics.

Blackouts are periods of total memory loss without the person having been unconscious or even drunk. During the "blackout" many normal or "abnormal" actions may have taken place, but all memory for them is lost. They may last for one or two days or possibly longer.

With all of these criteria, which ones should determine whether or not a patient is alcoholic or "merely" on the road to becoming one? The answer lies in asking questions about withdrawal and tolerance phenomena which are *prima facie* evidence of addiction. A person can be alcoholic and never had D.T.s. Other withdrawal symptoms such as morning "shakes" can be present. These shakes occur after someone who has consumed a lot of alcohol (and is addicted to it) sleeps for some time and his blood alcohol level goes down. He awakens with severe shaking of the limbs, almost as gross as the tremors in D.T.s. The usual action taken by the alcoholic is to drink more alcohol to stop the shaking. The "shakes" are probably incipient D.T.s, but the symptoms have not yet progressed that far. If a patient admits to getting the shakes in the morning after heavy drinking the previous evening, he should be classified as an alcoholic if he meets at least one major and one minor criteria.

Tolerance is another matter. Some alcoholics will brag about their ability to "hold" their liquor without showing behavioral effects of intoxication. They may also be asked whether they can "hold" their liquor better than most of their peer groups and how much they can drink. The consumption of one fifth of a gallon of alcohol daily or for more than one day is evidence of alcoholism. Peer group characteristics can be misleading since the entire peer group can be either alcoholics or incipient alcoholics.

## ALCOHOLIC HALLUCINATIONS

Sometimes alcoholics get visual and auditory hallucinations without being psychotic otherwise, and *without* signs of an acute or chronic organic brain syndrome. This is called alcoholic hallucinosis and can occur while drinking or in withdrawal. Here the distinction must be made between an alcoholic schizophrenic and an alcoholic who is hallucinating. History and familiarity with schizophrenic "thought disorders" will sometimes make diagnosis possible. A good question to ask is if the patient has ever experienced hallucinations without alcohol in close temporal proximity to the onset of the hallucinations. (The time period between hallucinations and alcohol consumption should be longer than ten to fourteen days, otherwise the hallucinations can still result from incipient D.T.s.) If the patient hallucinates after a two-week absence of alcohol he may be schizophrenic or have another psychosis, or *still* possibly have incipient D.T.s, but this is rather unlikely.

## KORSAKOFF'S PSYCHOSIS

This is a variety of *chronic* brain syndrome that occurs after very long-standing abuse of alcohol. It is rare to see one of the victims of this disease outside of a hospital. Korsakoff's psychosis is characterized by the usual signs of organic brain syndrome plus a specific and peculiar type of memory impairment which causes the patient to confabulate. Confabulation is the term used to describe the filling in or memory gaps with plausible sounding (to the patient) stories. For example, if you ask the patient if he has met you before, he may say he has (althought in reality he has not) and proceed to give you details of when and where, if you ask him. In general, patients who have memory gaps in other organic brain syndromes will say that they cannot remember.

Confabulation seems to be almost exclusively confined to this type of alcoholic syndrome. Along with the psychosis there are neurological deficits in the sensation of touch, especially in the lower limbs. This causes the patient to walk peculiarly, by slapping his feet to the ground so he can tell where they are.

To review then for a moment. The major criteria for the diagnosis of alcoholism are divided into two groups; physical and psychological dependence. Evidence of physical dependence is: 1) tolerance, which is defined as being able to ingest enough alcohol to reach a blood level of 150 mg./100 cc *without gross evidence* of *intoxication.* You can estimate this by asking the patient if he seems to be able to drink much more than his peers without getting drunk. If you suspect the peer group of being alcoholic ask how much alcohol he can hold relative to someone whom he knows only drinks occasionally; 2) phenomena such as morning "shakes," hallucinosis, outright D.T.s, and blackouts. Evidence of psychological dependence consists of drinking in the face of strong medical and social constraints and the subjective impression that the patient has lost control of his alcohol consumption.

## WHAT TO DO IF YOUR PATIENT IS ALCOHOLIC

Alcoholism is an extraordinarily difficult problem to treat, as is any addiction. Alcohol, like other addicting CNS depressants, can be psychologically depressing. Very often it is a "chicken and egg" problem whether the depression preceded the drinking or vice versa. In my experience the vast majority of alcoholics are depressed. Unfortunately, antidepressants will not solve the problem once the addiction to alcohol has taken hold. Furthermore, antidepressants do not work as well if the person drinks on top of them. Most alcoholics should first be referred to a doctor for a physical checkup and should, as well, be referred to Alcoholics Anonymous. There are very many studies showing that individual psychotherapy is not as effective as AA. If the patient has sufficient psychopathology to warrant individual psychotherapy this should be carried out in conjunction with referral to AA.

# CHAPTER XIV

## *Amine Hypotheses*

This chapter is provided for those readers who are interested in a fuller understanding of the current *hypotheses* of drug action. Related to these hypotheses are the following classes of drugs: Antidepressants, lithium, phenothiazines, Reserpine and Alphamethyl dopa, L-DOPA, and amphetamines. (Note that *sedatives* and *sleeping-pills* are *not included*.)

Structural formulas are given for the purposes of comparison and need not be memorized.

There are three neurotransmitters presently *hypothesized* to be directly involved with the production of depression, mania, and schizophrenia. These are serotonin, norepinephrine, and dopamine. Serotonin is also known as 5-hydroxytryptamine or 5-HT. Norepinephrine and serotonin are thought to be more involved with the production of depression or mania, whereas dopamine is thought to be more involved with schizophrenia.

NEUROTRANSMITTERS

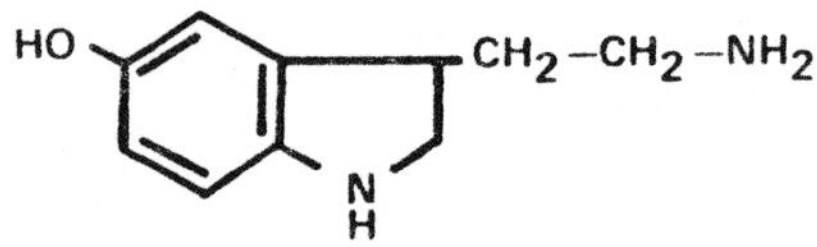

SEROTONIN (5-HT)

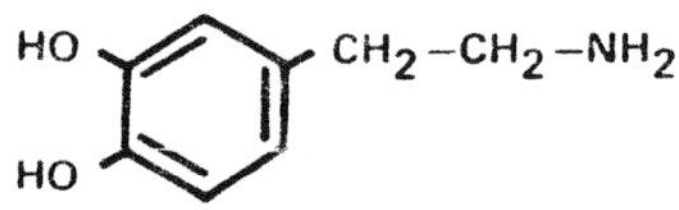

DOPAMINE

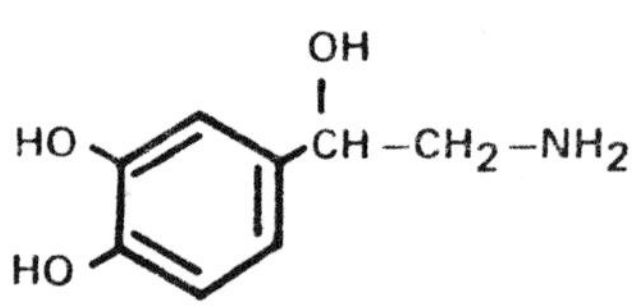

NOREPINEPHRINE

*Figure 1*

By neurotransmitter is meant that this is a naturally occurring substance in the brain cells and is released by the nerve cell when it is stimulated or fires by itself. It releases the neurotransmitter onto a receptor cell which also may fire, and so on, down the line. The neurotransmitters shown in Figure 1 are known to exist in groups of cells in specific locations throughout the brain. It is no wonder that these are thought to be associated with psychoses of various types since they look so similar to those drugs which we know are causes of temporary psychoses. Observe the similarities between these neurotransmitters and the drugs shown in Figure 2.

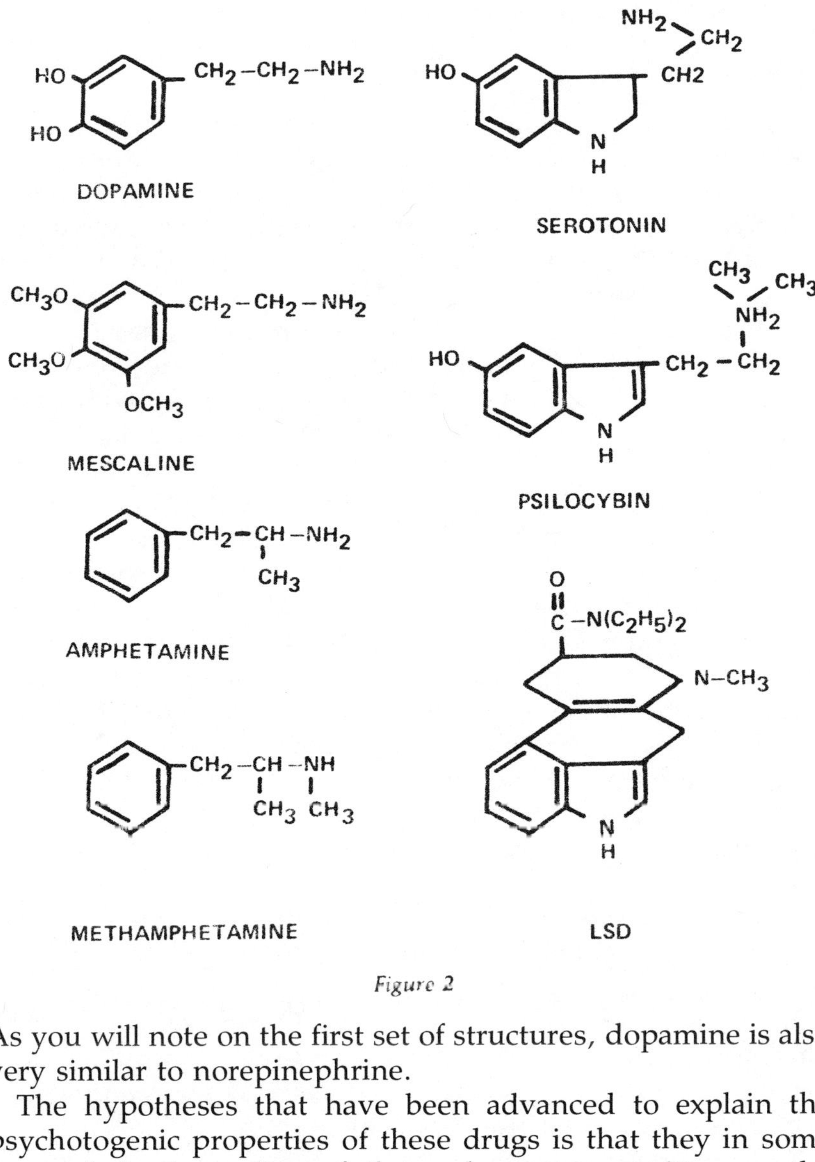


*Figure 2*

As you will note on the first set of structures, dopamine is also very similar to norepinephrine.

The hypotheses that have been advanced to explain the psychotogenic properties of these drugs is that they in some way mimic the action of the real neurotransmitter on the receptor cell and overstimulate it, or are sufficiently similar to be accepted by the receptor cell, but sufficiently dissimilar enough to cause the reactions we see. There are many investigators still looking for "natural" products of dopamine, norepinephrine or serotonin which the brains or bodies of psychiatric patients produce which would resemble these known psychotomimetic drugs and, hence, perhaps explain why the patient became psychotic.

In order for you to understand the basic mechanisms which are thought to operate in producing drug response, it is necessary to understand the following rather oversimplified principles of nerve cells and their receptors. The nerve cells which have those three neurotransmitters, store them in little granules or vesicles near the end membrane of the nerve cell. When the cell fires it releases the neurotransmitter from the vesicles into the cytoplasm of the firing cell and from there across the synaptic cleft onto the receptor. The space between the nerve cell and the receptor is known as the synaptic cleft and the whole complex (nerve cell, cleft, and receptor cell) is known as the synapse. Some of the transmitter (in the case of norepinephrine and dopamine) is immediately inactivated in the synaptic cleft by an enzyme known by the abbreviation COMT (catechol-O-methyl transferase). The rest of the neurotransmitter is either inactivated by the MAO (another enzyme, monoamine oxidase) in the receptor cell, or is taken back into the original nerve cell and stored again for future firing (reuptake). Some of the neurotransmitter is also inactivated by the MAO in the original nerve cell, both after it is released from the granules and after it is taken back (re-uptaken) by the cell. Figure 3 should aid visualization of the action.

There are several drugs which work by preventing or enhancing the re-uptake mechanism of the original firing cell. Other drugs deplete the granules of their supply, and still other drugs prevent the action of MAO and thereby increase the supply of neurotransmitter within the nerve cell. All three neurotransmitters are known chemically as monoamines but we need not be concerned about them here.

One hypothesis states, very concisely, and very roughly, that increased amounts of norepinephrine or serotonin in certain nerve cells or endings and ultimately, therefore, on the receptor cells will cause excitability and lead to mania. Decreased amounts of norepinephrine or serotonin however, will conversely lead to depression.

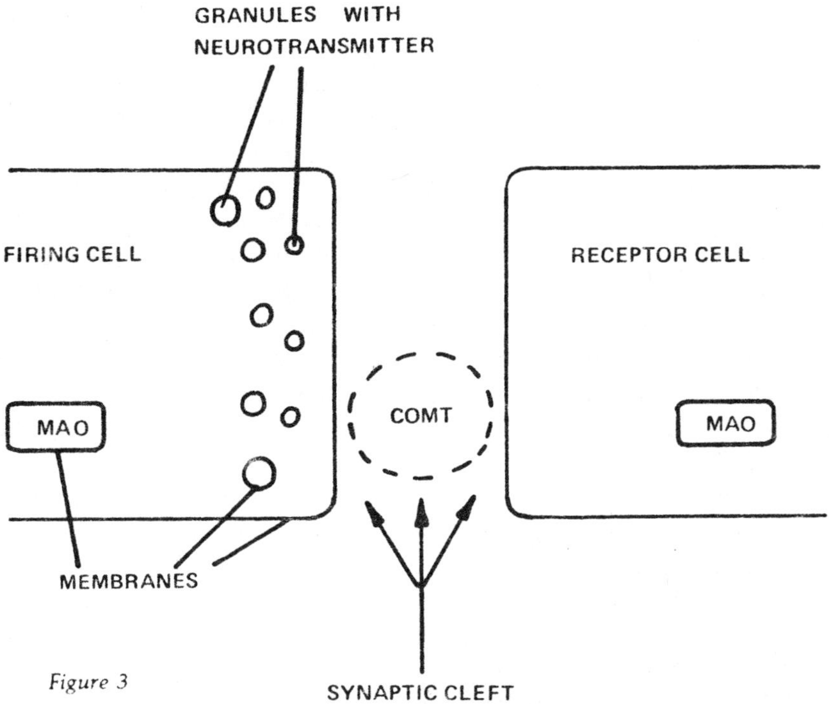


*Figure 3*

Another hypothesis concerning schizophrenia relates dopamine-containing neurons to schizophrenia because it is known that antipsychotic drugs produce "Parkinsonian" symptoms, always and inseparably (so far) from the antipsychotic agents' effects. Since it *is* known that Parkinson's Disease *results* from problems in the dopamine-containing neurons, they reason that antipsychotic drugs must also act upon not only *those* neurons producing Parkinsonian symptoms, but also on those neurons involved in the psychosis.

## DRUG ACTIONS: HYPOTHESES

Let us begin with those drugs which we know are antidepressants, either temporary (amphetamines) or more prolonged (tricyclics). As you can see by the structure of amphetamine it closely resembles both dopamine and norepinephrine. There is some thought that it produces excitement, good mood, and euphoria, and psychosis by releasing dopamine from its nerve endings. However, it is not destroyed by COMT in the synaptic cleft. It is also thought to release both norepinephrine and dopamine from the storage vesicles *and* to slightly inhibit MAO, thus preventing the termination of the action of both norepinephrine and dopamine. No wonder it is a *stimulant.* Since it resembles dopamine so closely, it is also though possible that it overstimulates the dopamine neurons in the same way as it causes overstimulation of norepinephrine neurons (by mimicry and release) and hence can lead to psychosis.

Tricyclics have been shown to inhibit the re-uptake mechanism, which is the most important way that cells terminate the action of the released neurotransmitter. Tricyclics are thought primarily to prevent the re-uptake of norepinephrine or serotonin and thus leave more of it on the receptor cell. This more continuous stimulation of the receptor by the released neurotransmitter is thought to be responsible for the increased mood.

MAO inhibitors, it is hypothesized, also can be responsible for increased mood by preventing the degradation and inactivation of the norepinephrine, thus leaving more of it both inside the firing cell and on the receptor cell.

As was noted, both tricyclics and MAO inhibitors take about two weeks to start working *behaviorally* or in terms of subjective mood. It is not clear yet why this is so. Lithium on the other side, being an antimanic drug, is though to *enhance* the re-uptake mechanism and prevent release of the neurotransmitter, norepinephrine, by doing something to the limiting membrane of the firing cell. Lithium also acts by increasing MAO activity* and hence, enhancing the degradation of norepinephrine. This action makes the antimanic action of lithium more comprehensible, but how it works to prevent depression is not explained by this action. Just how lithium can also work as an antidepressant in some manic-depressives is not clear from this explanation, in fact it

*Bockar, J. A., Increased human platelet MAO activity during Lithium Carbonate Therapy 1973.

should not be possible. Investigation has yet to clarify this paradox. Phenothiazines can cause the symptoms of dopamine *deficiency* which are called "Parkinsonian" symptoms, because persons with Parkinson's Disease are *known* to have a dopamine deficiency in certain areas of the brain. These areas are NOT responsible for the psychiatric symptomatology. However, because it is thought that phenothiazines must block the dopamine in these areas in order to produce "Parkinsonian" symptoms, they must also block the *dopamine neurons* in the areas which *are* responsible for psychotic psychiatric symptoms. The question is rightly asked therefore, "How come not all patients on phenothiazines get "Parkinsonian" side effects?" The answer lies probably in the dose and response curve of the entire population. Probably every patient taking phenothiazines would develop "Parkinsonian" side effects if the dose was high enough. Luckily, about 80% of patients treated have an antipsychotic effect from phenothiazines *without* having "Parkinsonian" side effects. This must say something about the sensitivity of the various receptors involved. In fact, some recent evidence indicates that there *are* two types of dopamine receptor-neurons (Klawans, 1973).

A word about L-DOPA. L-DOPA is given to patients with Parkinson's Disease to increase the amount of dopamine at the deficient sites in the brain. As you might expect, about 10 percent of the patients so treated get psychiatric symptomatology, ranging from psychosis to mania to depression. Psychosis might be easy to understand, given the above explanations. However, mania is also easily understandable if you know that dopamine can be converted to norepinephrine very easily, and it is excess norepinephrine which is thought to be responsible for mania. In the same way, drugs which block the conversion from dopamine to norepinephrine might be responsible for depression. Or further, drugs which resemble dopamine sufficiently to be converted to the norepinephrine-like compound might cause depression if they block the real norepinephrine. Such a drug is the common antihypertensive agent alphamethyl dopa (tradename: Aldomet). Aldomet can and does cause depression in about five to ten percent of persons treated with it who are evidently predisposed to depression to begin with. That predisposition is probably biological, but this is still hotly debated.

Reserpine, another antihypertensive drug, also causes severe depression in about 25% of those patients treated with it. It is known to deplete the norepinephrine storage granules of their supply of norepinephrine and this presumably leads to depression. Again, querying why all persons treated do not get depressed accents the incompleteness of our knowledge in this field.

# *References*

Detre, T.P. and Jarecki, H.G. *Modern Psychiatric Treatment,* Lippincott, Philadelphia, Pa., 1971.

Diagnostic and Statistical Manual of the American Psychiatric Association, 1980.

Freedman, A.M. and Kaplan, H.J. *Comprehensive Textbook of Psychiatry,* Williams & Wilkins, Baltimore, Md., 1967.

Harrison, T.R., et al. (eds.). *Principles of Internal Medicine,* McGraw-Hill, New York, 1974.

Klawans, H.L., Jr., "Pharmacology of Tardive Dyskinesis," *Amer. J. Psychiat.* 130:1 (January 1973).

Klein, D.F. and Davis, J.M. *Diagnosis and Drug Treatment of Psychiatric Disorders,* Williams & Wilkins, Baltimore, Md., 1969.

Lebensohm, Z.M. and Jenkins, R.B. "Improvement of Parkinsonism in depressed patients treated with ECT," *Amer. J. Psychiat.* 132:3 (March 1975).

National Commission on Marijuana and Drug Abuse. *"Marijuana, a Signal of Misunderstanding,"* New American Library, New York, 1972.

# Glossary

ACETYLCHOLINE: A known neurotransmitter in the peripheral nervous system and neurotransmitter of the parasympathetic nervous system which is a subgroup of peripheral nerves. Also hypothesized to be neurotransmitter in central nervous system.

AKATHISIA: A side effect of phenothiazines *and other* antipsychotic drugs: it is the subjective sensation of not being able to sit still; of having to move legs and feet particularly.

ANALGESIC: Pain relieving.

ANERGIA: Lack of energy.

ANGINA PECTORIS: A syndrome characterized by pain in the chest around the heart, occasionally profuse sweating and anxiety. It is usually associated with a real temporary deficit in blood supply to the heart muscle causing severe pain which often can be relieved by nitroglycerin tablets under the tongue.

ANOREXIA: Loss of appetite.

ANTICHOLINERGIC: Having properties which interfere with the functioning of the cholinergic (in most cases parasympathetic) nervous system.

BIPOLAR: In this text bipolar refers to persons with manic-depressive illness in either phase of that illness or having a history compatible with such a diagnosis.

CHOLINERGIC: Refers to nervous systems utilizing acetylcholine as their neurotransmitter—in this text primarily the parasympathetic nervous system.

CONFABULATION: A peculiar way of filling in gaps in memory by making up plausible-sounding but false stories; primarily seen in alcoholic brain disease.

CNS: Central nervous system: the brain and spinal cord.

CYCLOTHYMIC: Refers to type of personality in which the person tends to have mild depressions and mild elations as distinguished from manic-depressive illness where the mood swings are much more intense.

CNS DEPRESSANT: A drug which causes slowing or decrease in excitability of nerve cells in the CNS: all sleeping pills, narcotics, tranquilizers, and alcohol are CNS depressants.

DELUSION: A belief held by a person *which is not culturally* accepted and which cannot be changed by reasoning; a false belief.

EEG (electroencephalograph) Commonly known as brain wave test. A form of polygraph specifically designed to pick up frequencies of electromagnetic waves emitted by the brain.

EPINEPHRINE: A substance released by the adrenal gland which causes signs of sympathetic reaction.

HALLUCINATION: A sensory perception which has no basis in reality; may be visual, auditory, olfactory (smell) etc.

HYPERSOMNIA: Excessive sleeping —more than eight hours per night in an adult.

HYPERVENTILATION: Excessive breathing—usually too deep for too long a period of time; a syndrome consisting of numbness and tingling of the fingertips and toes bilaterally, chest pain and anxiety, due to overbreathing.

HYPNOTIC: Sleep producing—the medical term for sleep-producing drugs. drugs.

HYPOGLYCEMIA: Low blood sugar.

HYPOMANIA: A state of increased motor activity, excessively good mood; *not* psychotic, necessarily.

HYSTERICAL, HYSTERIA: Terms used to denote a neurotic condition wherein the person converts anxiety into physical symptoms and sometimes mental symptoms such as hysterical amnesia. The physical symptoms are varied but can be paralysis of a limb, blindness, etc. These physical or mental symptoms do not usually follow known anatomic pathways and can be removed under pentobarbital or hypnosis.

I.M.: Intramuscularly—refers to how a medicine is injected into a muscle.

ILLUSION: An incorrect sensory perception having some basis in reality as opposed to a hallucination. It is an illusion for example when the road looks wet in front of you because of the angle of the sun on it, when it is really dry.

ISCHEMIA: Insufficient blood supply.

MAOI: Monoamine oxidase inhibitor—type of antidepressant.

MANIA: A state of extreme increase in motor activity, verbal activity and euphoric or hostile mood; generally reserved for these symptoms in combination with psychosis.

MENTATION: Thinking or thought processes.

NARCOTIC: Producing numbness; usually also produce sleep or lethargy in moderate doses. Medically used as pain relievers.

NEURON: Nerve cell.

NOREPINEPHRINE: A neurotransmitter in the CNS and peripheral sympathetic nervous system.

OBS: Organic brain syndrome—deficits in memory and other intellectual functions due to disease or dysfunction of the neurons in the brain.

ORTHOSTATIC HYPOTENSION: Temporary decrease in blood pressure when person changes positions from sitting or lying down to standing. The person feels dizzy temporarily but returns to normal in a few seconds.

Generally a side effect of major tranquilizers and antidepressants.

PARASYMPATHETIC, NERVOUS SYSTEM: A part of peripheral nervous system concerned with vegetative functions.

PARESTHESIA: Numbness and tingling of the extremities—example when foot "falls asleep".

PATHOLOGIC INTOXICATION: A person who gets drunk with blackouts and possibly violent on one or two normal drinks.

PERISTALSIS: Consecutive constriction of intestinal segments pushing food along.

PHENOTHIAZINE: A major tranquilizing drug as opposed to minor tranquilizers.

PHYSIOLOGICAL: Refers to the process of the functioning of various *body* systems.

REM: Rapid eye movement stage of sleep.

SEDATIVE: Calming, quieting—a drug causing decrease in nervous excitement.

SOMATIC: Refers to the body as opposed to psychic referring to the mind.

SYMPATHETIC NERVOUS SYSTEM: Part of the peripheral nervous system as well as certain connections in the CNS—responsible for "fight or flight" reactions and general body homeostasis.

TOLERANCE: The physiological process whereby the user of a drug can tolerate physically more drug than is usual to produce the desired effect. Tolerance implies the need to increase the dose of a drug in order to keep obtaining the desired response. Cross tolerance occurs when drugs with similar effects produce tolerance to all those drugs with similar effects, e.g., if a person is tolerant to barbiturates he may also be tolerant to nonbarbiturate sleeping pills.

TOXIC: Poisonous; a state of mind or body resulting from poisonous drug or excessive dosage of medicines or endogenous toxins.

TREMOR: Fine or coarse shaking of limbs, generally hands.

TRICYCLIC: A type of antidepressant.

UNCINATE FITS: Another synonym for psychomotor epilepsy or temporal lobe epilepsy. In this condition the patient has violent outbursts of rage which last a few minutes to hours.

UNIPOLAR: In this text refers to a type of depression generally formerly called endogenous depression, characterized by weight loss, sleep loss, and agitation.

## Glossary of Drugs

| Generic Name | Brand | Company |
|---|---|---|
| | **Major Tranquilizers (Antipsychotic Agents)** | |
| **Phenothiazines** | | |
| Acetophenazine | Tindal | Schering |
| Butaperazine | Repoise | Robins |
| Carphenazine | Proketazine | Wyeth |
| Chlorpromazine | Thorazine | Smith, Kline & French |
| Dixyrazine | Esucos | Union Chimiques Belge* |
| Fluphenazine | Prolixin, Permitil | Squibb, White |
| Mesoridazine | Serentil | Boehringer Ingelheim |
| Methotrimeprazine | Levoprome | Lederle |
| Perphenazine | Trilafon | Schering |
| Piperacetazine | Quide | Dow Pharmaceutical |
| Prochlorperazine | Compazine | Smith, Kline & French |
| Promazine | Sparine | Wyeth |
| Propericiazine | Neuleptil | Rhone-Poulenc* |
| Thiazinamium | Multergan | Rhone-Poulenc* |
| Thiethylperazine | Torecan | Boehringer Ingleheim |
| Thioproperazine | Majeptil | Rhone-Poulenc* |
| Thioridazine | Mellaril | Sandoz |
| Trifluoperazine | Stelazine | Smith, Kline & French |
| Triflupromazine | Vesprin | Squibb |
| **Butyrophenones** | | |
| Dehydrobenzperidol | Innovar | McNeil |
| Haloperidol | Haldol | McNeil |
| **Thioxanthenes** | | |
| Chlorprothixene | Taractan | Roche |
| Thiothixene | Navane | Pfizer Roerig |
| **Reserpines** | | |
| Deserpidine | Harmonyl | Abbott |
| Rescinnamine | Moderil | Pfizer |
| Reserpine | Serpasil and others | Ciba and others |
| | **Antidepressants** | |
| **Tricyclics** | | |
| Amitriptyline | Elavil | Merck |
| Desipramine | Pertofrane, Norpramin | USV Pharmaceitucal Geigy, Lakeside |

## Glossary of Drugs (cont.)

| Generic Name | Brand | Company |
|---|---|---|
| Imipramine | Tofranil | Geigy |
| Nortriptyline | Aventyl | Lilly |
| Protriptyline | Vivactil | Merck |
| Trimipramine | Surmontil | Rhone-Poulenc |
| **MAO Inhibitors** | | |
| Etryptamine | Monase (withdrawn) | Upjohn |
| Iproniazid | Marsilid (withdrawn) | Roche |
| Isocarboxazid | Marplan | Roche |
| Mebanazine | Actomol | Imperial Chemical Industry |
| Pargyline | Eutonyl | Abbott |
| Phenelzine | Nardil | Warner |
| Pheniprazine | Catron (withdrawn) | Lakeside |
| Tranylcypromine | Parnate | Smith, Kline & French |
| **Prescribable Stimulants** | | |
| Amphetamine | Benzedrine | Smith, Kline & French |
| Dextro-Amphetamine | Dexedrine | Smith, Kline & French |
| Deanol | Deaner | Riker |
| Methamphetamine | Desoxyn | Abbott |
| Methylphenidate | Ritalin | Ciba |
| | **Nonbarbiturate Minor Tranquilizers and Sedatives** | |
| Chlordiazepoxide | Librium | Roche |
| Chlormethazanone | Trancopal | Sterling-Winthrop |
| Diazepam | Valium | Roche |
| Hydroxyzine | Vistaril, Atarax | Pfizer, Roerig |
| Meprobamate | Miltown, Equanil | Wallace, Wyeth |
| Oxazepam | Serax | Wyeth |
| | **Nonbarbiturate Sleeping Pills (Hypnotics)** | |
| Ethchlorvynol | Placidyl | Abbott |
| Ethinamate | Valmid | Dista |
| Flurazepam | Dalmane | Roche |
| Glutethimide | Doriden | Ciba, USV Pharmaceutical |
| Methaqualone | Quaalude | Rorer |
| Methyprylon | Noludar | Roche |

# Index